MARTIN'S
MAGIC
MOTIVATION
BOOK

PHYLLIS MARTIN

MARTIN'S
MAGIC
MOTIVATION
BOOK

How to Become an
Anointed One
In Your Organization

ST. MARTIN'S PRESS | NEW YORK

Design by Victoria Hartman

First Edition

10 9 8 7 6 5 4 3 2 1

Library of Congress Cataloging in Publication Data

Martin, Phyllis Rodgers.
Martin's Magic motivation book.

1. Success in business. 2. Employee motivation.
I. Title. II. Title: Magic motivation book.
HF5386.M365   1984   650.1   84-13267
ISBN 0-312-51708-4 (pbk.)

"Aim So High You'll Never Be Bored" on page 17 is reprinted with permission from Harry J. Gray, Chairman and Chief Executive Officer, United Technologies, Box 360, Hartford, Ct. 06141.

The cartoon on page 73 is reprinted with permission from Brice Diedrick, Director of Licensing, Tribune Company Syndicate, Inc.

The material on pages 106–109 is reprinted with permission from *Chemical Engineering Progress* 77, no. 7 (July 1981): 23–24.

The signatures you see here are of those caring people who either contributed to this book or inspired my writing it. If I could I would add all the names of friends, mentors, and bosses from P & G days. Thanks all of you up to and including Edward G. Harness.

The circled signature is that of my husband, Bruce, whose contribution included word processing, editing, prodding, and large doses of understanding and encouragement.

Shirley Briggs

Bruce Martin

Jeanne L. Robertson

Sheryl L. Althaus

John H Sanders

Patricia Diehl

Sally Stivender

Vada Stanley

KIPP MARTIN

Larry H. Rigg

Jill A. Baker

Lois J. Otto

Jay Martin

Bob Braun

Barbara

Mary Caske Caldwell

Jacqueline A. Erwin

Annabelle Paul

Priscilla Petty

Eleanor T. Boehm

Ruth von Gelder Dave Dyer

Dr. Maureen Getz Rouse

Charles Beaty II

William C. Diehl

Mary W. Pewhert Don Carr

Judi Alise —Stu

Ken

Mort

Robin R. Sori

Edward Mandel

Nancy Schellhous SUE REINHART

Cynthia L. Muir

John Scudder Barbara J. Majors

Jean M. Plattner

Merlin R. James

Joyce C. Shewman

JoAnn Abel

Richelle Becker Mary F. Griffith

Wanda B. Mosbacker

CONTENTS

INTRODUCTION

The purpose of this book is to tell you how to become an "anointed one" in your organization.

The actual observation that certain men and women are "anointed"—that is, pegged for promotion—struck me years ago when I started my career at Procter & Gamble. Just as animals have a pecking order—or butting order—work groups spawn leaders and those leaders are clearly marked. Identified. Anointed. Even the delivery people can tell you who they are.

Why are the anointed ones destined to succeed?

Primarily because upper-level managers have a way of letting intermediate managers know which subordinates are viewed as comers. Consequently the intermediate managers pay more attention to developing these chosen ones.

Much has been written for and about these comers, fast-trackers, golden-haired ones. Not enough has been written about *how* to become an anointed one if the decision makers don't discover you on their own.

This then is a book for the bright, creative person who is willing to work for promotion but who also recognizes that *working for a promotion* is not enough. It is about *earned* advancement. There are already too many who get advancement without earning it; I've no desire to add to their number. I'm not going for *surface* power but rather for *staying* power.

I do not tout as talents dirty tricks, callousness, or manipulation.

I do provide a framework, an ethical compass, a concrete "how-to" outline for you. You do the work but I'll be with you every step of the way.

This is your personal seminar. I put it in book form because it's the only way I can reach many of you. I also put it in book form because I'd be foolish not to. My mentors have told me to put my motivational talks on paper, and my tormentors are asking for copies of my notes. Because I give as many as six talks a week—in addition to writing a job column and developing a job tip for my weekly television spot—I do have something to say.

Please consider what I say seriously and consider all of it. While it's fine to jump around a bit, to land on the most intriguing topics first, don't skip any of it. Each segment is necessary, otherwise I wouldn't have included it.

If you immerse yourself fully, you can expect results within the first week. If you will absorb a chapter each week, by ten weeks from today you should see specific, dramatic results, such as:

- more power in your present position
- recognition from those in power
- a promotion or promise of one
- a significant increase in salary or earnings
- an offer of a new position

Continue the program and you will become the "anointed one."

Part I
SELF-MOTIVATION

1

THE WELL-GROOMED MIND

Before we talk about your role in the next ten weeks that could change your life, I'd like to at least mention the employer's side.

And the message from management, particularly top management, is that there is room at the top despite overcrowding below. Indeed, a great search is on to discover the superstars.

Your job, then, is to convey this message: "I have not only goals but also the ability and the desire—make that drive—to carry them out. Furthermore, I'm dedicating myself to developing the best that's in me because I'm top-drawer material." This is, of course, a sales campaign. And as in every well-planned campaign, you must assess the product being sold: YOU.

Let's start with a self-assessment of the very essence of you—your personality. To put it simply, your personality is the effect you produce as the result of what you are.

Can you change the effect you produce? Yes.

Because you have a great deal of control over your habits and actions, you can organize your mental equipment. You can develop a well-groomed mind. That's what this first chapter is about. It's the first step and the one that establishes the direction of your campaign. Study this chapter seriously for at least one week. Put yourself into every sentence; I need your cooperation, not just your presence.

THE *MAR*TECHNIQUE FOR OVERCOMING IQ TRAPS

The **Mar**technique is a clear, concise method for developing the well-groomed mind. And a well-groomed mind is the first requisite for the upward bound.

What is a well-groomed mind? It's an uncluttered mind. One that is in superb working order.

How do you unclutter a mind? Take a **Q** from me.

Let me back up a bit. I became fascinated with the letter *Q* because my brother, whose middle name was Quincy, used to tell me that *Q* was the most overlooked letter in the alphabet. Further, he said, "If you ever want to commit anything to memory, find a '*Qt*' way to say it to yourself. Trim away all the other clutter, use the *Q* as a symbol, and it will stay with you forever."

It works.

I'll demonstrate: I became interested in IQs because as a child I thought my brother invented the term. The symbol continued to fascinate me even after I learned that IQ stood for "Intelligence Quotient."

I was still impressed by IQs when I went to work for Procter & Gamble. And I had a "whoopee" reaction when I became an employment supervisor and learned I could use what we termed "mental alertness" tests in evaluating potential employees.

My honeymoon with the mental alertness test was short-lived. I learned that mental alertness—or, if you insist, IQ—was only one predictor of success on the job. And it wasn't a very good one.

What to do? I was still enchanted with the letter *Q*, so I developed the idea of looking for "Questians" to hire. A

Questian is someone who considers work a quest. A Questian has an Inner Quest IQ.

When I first discussed my findings with our company psychologist, his reactions were—in this order—horror, hilarity, and finally something resembling humility.

As his horror lessened and the laughter subsided, he told me, "Your work will never make a scholarly publication."

"Is it too simple?" I asked.

"Actually, it's simply wonderful and the soundest thing I've seen. Wish I'd developed it," he answered.

Now then, if you're wondering whether a high IQ is important for upward mobility, I'll answer yes. But my yes refers to a high Inner Quest IQ.

Before we study the Inner Quest IQ, let's study the undesirable or less than ideal IQs. Try to spot yourself in some of them. When you do, consider ways to modify or change the behavior that lands you there. Don't be too hard on yourself. It's important to realize that most of us pass through many phases or stages before we can hope to reach the most desirable type of IQ, the Inner Quest.

Here are some of the IQs I've discovered.

THE "INSTANT QUENCH"
IQ

The person with the Instant Quench personality wants everything right now.

An Instant Quench personality is usually:

immoderate
impulsive
inconsistent
indulgent (of self)
imprudent
imbalanced
indiscreet
indiscriminate
impudent
inconstant
insouciant
inveigling

incendiary (incites others
  to extreme action)
indelicate
instinctively an instigator
irrepressible
impatient
impermanent
impetuous
improvident
intemperate
inquisitive
in debt
irresistible

How to Overcome the Instant Quench IQ

Ask yourself these basic questions:

1. "Will it matter at this time next year whether I do—or have—the thing that seems so important today? Five years from now? Will I, in the long run, consider it worth the price?"

2. "Is my eagerness to act causing me to spring ideas in the wrong setting and to the wrong people: causing me to race too fast for normal working conditions?"

It's first necessary to identify the "instant quench" traits in your personality before you can motivate yourself to make changes.

Because the Instant Quench person is irrepressible and often irresistible, a complete change is *not* in order. Irrepressibility, for example, is actually *enthusiasm that needs a sense of direction*. Once the Instant Quench person harnesses the enthusiasm by setting goals—and sticking to the goals—that person is moving toward the desirable Inner Quest personality.

And being inquisitive is often the underlying trait of the innovator. While it is necessary to channel the inquisitiveness, there is no need to stifle it.

The incendiary quality of the Instant Quencher can also become sheer *drive,* an important quality for the results-oriented, upward-bound person.

Examine each of the traits listed; admit to those that describe you; then vow to modify or rid yourself of those that impede your progress. You might ask someone who knows you well to help in your evaluation. Such an independent affirmation will help you to make a true assessment. The practice and patience required to do all this will lead you to a more solid, and winning, personality.

THE "I QUIT"
IQ

The I Quit person often threatens to quit but seldom makes good on the promise. This person rarely finishes projects, so in terms of contribution he or she has already quit.

The I Quit personality is usually:

inert

indecisive

insular

ill-natured

inclined toward criticism

immune to iffy propositions

ill-boding (makes dire predictions designed to discourage the contributors)

ignorant of valid opportunities

intent on systematically destroying the illusions of others

How to Overcome the I Quit IQ

Ask yourself:

1. "How will my organization fare if I really do quit?"
2. "Will my contributions to its progress be missed?"

Do your answers reveal that you're not a contributor? Indeed, that you threaten to quit because you've never belonged?

If so, begin today to start a program of reconciliation. This reconciliation must first take the form of self-healing, for clearly something is very wrong if you are always casting yourself in the I Quit mold. After taking yourself in hand, force yourself to rededicate yourself to your field of work and to your organization.

Consider this policy of one of the most prestigious career counseling firms around: A candidate must *improve* his position *within* his present company *before* the counselor will consider him for outside referral.

Instead of threatening to quit, review your present position. Actually write out a list of your responsibilities. Next make a renewed effort to carry out those responsibilities. Third—when the time is right, perhaps at a regularly scheduled employee appraisal session—say to your boss, "Here is my view of my job and the way I believe my responsibilities should be carried out, but I want your suggestions." Then, listen without resentment or interruption to what comes next.

I do not advise the I Quit person to initiate an interview with the boss. This is too dangerous *at this stage* and could result in your boss's accepting the resignation you haven't actually tendered.

You have much to gain by leaving the I Quit mold:

• You will undoubtedly strengthen your present position.

• You have the option of quitting if you so desire—with the assurance of a positive send-off, complete with good references.

• You have not slammed the door on yourself should you wish to return.

• You are on your way to becoming an Inner Quest person.

THE "I QUIBBLE"
IQ

The I Quibble personality is characterized by quibbling questions. The I Quibble person loves to attend meetings because this affords the opportunity to quibble with the moderator about a point of order.

The I Quibble personality is usually:

irritable
irrelevant
intent on the inconsequential
  and immaterial
irksome
irascible
itching to be heard

questioning
quarrelsome
querulous
quick to quantify and
  qualify everything while
  missing the quintessential
  qualities

How to Overcome the I Quibble IQ

Ask yourself this question:

"Is it possible that I enjoy finding fault?"

If you answer yes, try listing the "positives" you observe the next time you're in a group situation. Give yourself a quota, say, three positive observations. There's no need to mention these aloud unless your mentioning them contributes substance to what is going on. Your *doing* this is the important factor. With a bit of practice, you'll develop the habit of a positive outlook (so necessary to your success).

THE "I QUAKE"
IQ

Most of us have experienced tremors of the I Quake personality.

The I Quake personality is usually:

insecure
inhibited
immobile
introspective
introverted
indecisive
imbued with an inferiority
   complex
inclined to seek invisibility

inarticulate, indistinct,
   and almost inaudible
   (mumbling is a
   characteristic)
quivering
queasy
quailing
a quagmire of qualms and
   uncertainty
always in a quandary

The inferiority complex is the common denominator of the I Quake personality.

How to Overcome the I Quake IQ

Remind yourself that you have a solid contribution to make, otherwise you wouldn't have been hired in the first place.

Also give some weight to this fact: Just about everybody has an inferiority complex about something.

An inferiority complex is almost a common denominator in the people department. This fact hit me with force early in my career as a counselor, for at some point in almost every counseling session I would hear a remark such as, "You don't realize this, Mrs. Martin, but I have this terrible inferiority complex."

This admission is so frequent I've come to expect it. And, if I'm not careful, I have to stop myself before I blurt, "So what else is new?"

Trust me when I tell you that nurturing an inferiority complex is a selfish act. The person who quakes—or is *self*-conscious—is selfish. To be self-conscious means to be conscious of self. You can climb out of the I Quake trap by becoming *other*-conscious. Forget yourself enough to be yourself. Then go about developing your consciousness of others—of focusing on the needs and views of other people. Not only will you stop quaking, you'll forget you ever did.

THE "IDOL (ALSO SPELLED IDLE) QUOTE"
IQ

You can spot the Idol Quote personality by the id*ol* quotes, id*le* quotes, and rubber-stamp words. The Idol Quote person overcomes feelings of inferiority by seeking security in the words and ideas of idols.

The Idol Quote personality is usually:

imitative
impressionable
an impersonator
incapable of creative thought
   or expression

imbued with an inexhaustive supply of jargon and canned phrases

How to Overcome the Idol Quote IQ

Try this method: Look at several of your memos and letters. Then spot the words, phrases, and ideas you've borrowed. Next, paraphrase each piece of writing using sparkling, original words in place of the borrowed ones. Make this paraphrasing of your work a habit.

If only some of our politicians would do this, we wouldn't be stuck with tired phrases such as "at this point in time" or "meaningful dialogue."

Anyway, I promise that if you put this paraphrasing idea into practice, others will begin to read what you write and to listen when you talk.

THE "INNER QUIRK"
IQ

The Inner Quirk personality is the most common IQ type. All of us spend some time loitering in the throes of our inner quirks. Change is so difficult, and as one woman who personifies this IQ type said with unpardonable pride, "That's just the way I am."

The Inner Quirk personality:

• Is easily sidetracked and deals with derivatives and side isues instead of basics.

• Carries a grudge. Such a person wastes time and energy in hating and doesn't realize that hating is a form of mental halitosis.

• Gripes. Finds fault with people and things. Thinks people are finding fault with him or her.

• Uses energy to resist change instead of channeling the change in a constructive way.

• Is self-centered rather than other-centered. Thus, he or she spends unnecessary time in wondering what others think of her or him, and so loses emotional balance (poise). As a result, he or she talks too much or too little.

• Is mastered by irritations instead of mastering irritations.

• Is accident-prone.

• Is often a hypochondriac.

• Spends an inordinate amount of time in regretting; doesn't realize that life cannot be lived retroactively.

• Thinks that good things happen to other people. And why shouldn't they? If there are 234,883,707 persons in the United States alone and you are only one of them, naturally more good things will happen to the other 234,883,706. There are more of them.

How to Overcome the Inner Quirk IQ

Recognize that quirks become habits and an ingrained part of our personalities. An Inner Quirk personality is marked for failure. Indeed, 65 percent of all firings, maybe more, are due to personality defects; i.e., "not getting along with others." This is true, no matter what the formal discharge papers say.

What to do?

If you would be marked for success, instead of failure, examine and try to *emulate* the Inner Quest Personality.

THE "INNER QUEST" PERSONALITY

The Inner Quest person usually has a dream. Realists call it a goal, but it's a dream nonetheless. The Inner Quest person is the creative person or the innovator.

The Inner Quest personality:

• **Has a lifetime goal.** Seems willing to go at the goal a day at a time, but the larger goal is always there.

• Is willing to pay a price in order to achieve the goal.

• Knows the importance of being noticed—in a nice way. And when noticed, is worth noticing—rewards the noticer with a noteworthy view.

• Doesn't traffic in trivialities. Is a constructive, not a destructive, worrier.

• Makes use of tranquilizing periods, not pills.

• Is forward looking; looks forward to everything. Has no regrets over what might have been. Knows that we can't change even five minutes of the past.

• Is a deep listener. Hears not just the words but the message.

• Communicates clearly in writing, in person, and on the telephone.

• Respects and accepts responsibility.

• Knows how to assign values to assignments. Hence is able to do assignments in the order of their importance.

• Develops sensitivity to others without being overly sensitive. Seldom gets "hurt feelings."

• Has imagination and broad vision.

• Encourages the positive characteristics of others.

• Takes responsibility for the mistakes of subordinates while giving them credit for their accomplishments.

• Is a self-rewarder as well as a self-starter.

• Is made better, not bitter, by rejection.

• Is always underpaid; i.e., makes sure he or she is never overpaid by contributing more in value than money received.

• Promises everything later than it can be delivered, thereby being always ahead of schedule.

• Observes trends without being trendy. Is a channel for constructive change.

• Has a youthful outlook. Knows the signs attributed to age, such as excess booze, excess weight, and too much emphasis on "how things used to be."

• Uses recreation to recreate.

• Is not constrained by the job title.

• Clears the path of promotion by learning about the job ahead and training a subordinate as a successor.

• Keeps supervisor informed about goals, about what is going on in his or her particular field, about the progress of work, and about major accomplishments and major goofs.

• Has a sense of direction. UP.

• Is energetic.

The Inner Quest person never adds to a problem but is always part of the solution to problems. The Inner Quest peson has gone beyond "Who am I?" and is more concerned with "Whose am I?" and "How can I serve?"

Aim So High You'll Never Be Bored

The
greatest waste
of our
natural resources
is the
number of
people
who never
achieve their
potential.
Get out
of that
slow lane.
Shift
into that
fast lane.
If you think
you can't,
you won't.
If you think
you can,
there's a
good chance
you will.
Even making
the effort
will make
you feel
like a new
person.
Reputations
are made
by searching
for things that
can't be done
and doing them.
Aim low:
boring.
Aim high:
soaring.

2
COMING TO YOUR SENSES:
ALL FIVE OF THEM

It is through our senses that we send messages to each other. Advertisers and salespeople know all about stimulating the sense organs in order to promote and sell a product.

Often we, as individuals, overlook the power of the senses in determining and developing our attractiveness to others. We tend to think personal chemistry, or charisma, is just there. That it cannot be acquired.

It can.

You can change a shaky, unattractive self-image into a positive, self-assured image.

How?

By being sensitive as well as sensible. By coming to your senses—all five of them.

SIGHT: THE FIRST FILTER

Let's start with the sense of sight; everyone else does. Sight is the first filter all of us use to screen out what seems undesirable.

Unless we recognize the name of a motel, restaurant, or store, we judge it by what we see. Often, no other investigation is made.

18

What do others see when they look at you? An outstandingly attractive person? Or are you cast aside after five seconds as someone of little importance?

Mary Jane Flege, image consultant, says, "Sixty-five percent of what we say about ourselves is transmitted by our clothes and body language. It's not fair but that's how it is."

My experience bears out Mary Jane's observations. We judge others in a fleeting glance, so why scream "foul" when we're judged as quickly? Unfortunately, those fleeting glances make lasting impressions.

As a career consultant, I've worked with as varied a group of people as you're apt to find: Members of a motorcycle gang, prostitutes, ex-offenders, handicapped people, high-school students, college students, retired persons, unemployed and employed persons up to and including a company president and a board chairman. This I know: *No matter what job you hold or hope to hold, there is an outfit for success. Wear it and you've won a major campaign in the battle to move yourself forward.*

For corporate success, I suggest you learn to be an authority on your own best style and develop a practical but *distinctive* wardrobe. Clones don't do well in the corporate climb.

While today's executive man won't want to be cast in the John Molloy "mold," he can still benefit from studying *Molloy's Live for Success* (see Bibliography) and by reading Mr. Molloy's current newspaper columns.

The man's minimum basic wardrobe should include at least two quality suits of natural fibers or a blend that includes natural fibers, a jacket that coordinates with either suit, two pairs of business shoes (skip the tassels), a classic topcoat, a leather briefcase, six shirts of cotton or cotton blend fabric, six conservative ties, and a watch that is serviceable as well as handsome. The coordinating jacket is not for wear during *normal* business hours unless it is part of the standard dress code and unless such a jacket is also worn by people of power within the organization. Do take into account the dress code (whether it is written or "understood").

Although stripes and subdued "shadow plaids" are in style, some judgment must be used in their selection. A good test is this one: If someone who is across the room from you—let's say, about fifteen feet or more away—can discern the pattern, it's too strong.

The executive woman—or the woman on the way to becoming an executive—today gives vent to her desire for an individual look. Despite a recent trend toward dresses as an option for business wear, suits remain the number one choice. Coordinates (especially two-piece dress outfits) are gaining favor and so is the coat dress. The woman who travels is still going to make suits the staple of her wardrobe, for very practical reasons: she can tuck an extra blouse or two inside a "carry-on" bag and be ready for any occasion.

A woman must give more thought to her clothing purchases than her male counterpart; in fact, until she—and her wardrobe—is established she will have to be very stern with herself. A bit of goal setting for the establishment of that wardrobe is in order.

You might try this method. Make three separate columns on a large piece of paper. In column one, make a list of desirable/desired items for the minimum, but smashing, wardrobe. In column two, make a list of items you now own that meet the standards you hope to establish: distinctive, becoming, appropriate. Subtract from list number one the items that make up list two. The difference consists of what you need to buy in order to arrive at the smashing wardrobe you hope to own. That difference makes up column three. Now for the real trick: *Do not buy any items that are not listed in the third column.* If need be, commit to memory Martin's Magic Maxim of Purchases:

> *Most of us could afford to buy almost anything we needed if we hadn't already spent the money for something we didn't.*

Look at my sample lists on pages 21–23 and then force yourself to do something similar. I promise this will prevent your making costly mistakes in the purchase of clothing. Remember, nothing is "a bargain" if it doesn't fit *your* needs.

The man's lists will of course be different but the same principles apply.

COLUMN ONE:

Minimum Basic Wardrobe

all-weather coat with zip-out lining (styled to fit over suits)

two skirted suits (of natural fibers or blend of natural fibers)

one two-piece dress (of a design to coordinate with other garments)

two basic dresses (if one of these is a coat dress, you'll have more flexibility in your wardrobe)

six blouses

two pairs basic pumps

one jacket (should coordinate with at least two other outfits)

briefcase

folding umbrella (same color as briefcase)

two handbags (my preference is for the handbag or purse that is designed to fit inside the briefcase)

shawl (a very "with it" and practical item)

two scarves

detachable dickey that can be inserted in order to change the neckline of dresses

COLUMN TWO:

Garments Now Owned
*(Must meet standards of desired wardrobe
and be in top condition.)*

lightweight raincoat
cashmere topcoat
teal suit
gray gabardine coat dress
teal blouse
beige blouse
white blouse
maroon blouse
two-piece Jacquard dress
maroon shoes
gray briefcase
gray folding umbrella
black handbag
maroon handbag
scarf

COLUMN THREE:

Need to Buy in Order to Complete
Basic Minimum Wardrobe
*(Carry a list such as this with you and refer to it
before making purchases.)*

all-weather coat with zip-out lining (this is not *now* a priority
  item because I own two basic coats but I shall look for a
  good buy—and I will settle only for a coat that is styled to
  fit over my suits)
gray or slate-blue suit (preferably collarless or with mandarin
  collar)
basic black dress

white blouse
gray or slate-blue blouse
one pair gray or black shoes
jacket
scarf
detachable dickey

Note to anyone entering the work force within the year: Make your basic wardrobe list *now* and resolve that every future purchase will meet your new guidelines. Show your list to those who love you and ask that birthday, Christmas, anniversary, graduation, or other gifts be made with an eye toward helping you to achieve a positive image.

All garments should fit well and be constructed of quality fabrics. Classic-styled clothing of good quality is an investment and should be so regarded.

I do not agree with "experts" who tell you *everything* must be made of natural fibers and I do not exclude garments made with the *newer* polyesters and other synthetics. In fact, after some of my on-the-road experiences with all-wool, all-cotton, all-silk garments, I've been ready to invest in a polyester farm.

Smart shoppers consider upkeep a necessary factor in the appearance of a garment and read all "instructions for care" labels *before* purchase. Those three little words, "Dry clean only," can add several dollars per wearing to the price of a blouse.

Man or woman, no matter what your occupation, there is a standard, perhaps even an ideal "look." Find out what it is and achieve it. You've hit upon the successful solution of what to wear—the appropriate uniform for your position—if your clothes meet this test: your employer could use you as the organizational model and would benefit by having everyone in the organization imitate your style (i.e. dress as you dress). If you're a banker, you might ask yourself if you typify the ideal banker in appearance? If an attorney, do you typify the ideal attorney? If you're a freelancer, do you typify (on sight) the best consultant, accountant, or designer? If your job involves inspecting construction, do you wear safety shoes?

If you're truly determined to pass that damned "first filter" with high marks, add to all the above a technique I call "enhancement." Enhancement is going beyond the basics and having the most attractive "you" emerge. I use this technique with discouraged job seekers. The dramatic results continue to amaze me. Perhaps the heightened self-confidence it engenders does the trick; I'm honestly not sure. I *am* sure it works.

Here are some examples:

If you want to seem healthier, I suggest
• having your teeth cleaned regularly and having any missing teeth replaced (this is a *must*)
• practicing good posture
• replacing a shuffle with a gait that suggests energy
• getting into a fitness program (if you are not already following a regimen)
• getting about five minutes of sun or sunlamp time—just enough to impart a healthy glow—if you're to make an important presentation or attend a meeting that's important to your future

If you want to appear taller, I suggest
• keeping the heels of your shoes in good repair
• using those padded heel inserts inside your shoes (best place to find them is the shoe store)
• wearing clothing with lines and patterns that go up and down, not across

If you want to appear more slender, I suggest
• wearing a jacket that is the same color as your trousers or skirt (sorry, but the dark shades are more slenderizing)

- avoiding chunky shoes
- pinking the bottom edge of your shirt or blouse so that when it's tucked in you'll have a smoother line
- wearing a watchband that is the same color as your outfit so that when your arms are at your side you don't call attention to your width
- carrying a slender attaché case or handbag (never both)

If you want that "clean-cut" look, I suggest
- having your hair professionally styled and, if you insist on a beard, having it professionally trimmed
- trimming (with a pair of sterile surgical scissors) excess hair from nose and ears
- having your eyebrows shaped or trimmed

If you want to appear younger, I suggest
- avoiding clothes that are too juvenile (this calls attention to your age)
- wearing up-to-the-minute but not "far-out" glasses frames
- wearing colors that are becoming to you (not colors that drain you or make you look drab)
- having a contemporary, but becoming, hairstyle

Finally, if you want to pass that first filter of screening, avoid: sunglasses worn indoors, smoking at important meetings, chewing gum, dangling threads, dandruff on the shoulders of your suit or dress, a dress that is longer than the coat with which it's worn, toothpicks, tattoos, and bow ties (on men).

SOUND ADVICE

Your vocal image—the way you sound—either contributes to or detracts from a positive personal image.

For some, therapy is necessary. If the problem is medical, seek medical advice. If the matter is merely cosmetic, and a regional accent or mumbling is causing problems for you, see a speech therapist.

I can't hear you; but if you're smart, you'll check with someone who can. You'll find out whether your voice—the way you sound—is creating sound barriers.

Immediate Help

I *can* suggest two dramatic ways for you to improve your communicating skills. And, you can do it in the time it takes for you to read the next few pages.

Listening

The first concerns listening. If you would be a glistening conversationalist, learn to listen.

Study the word *glistening*. Remind yourself that the biggest part of the word is listening. **G**listening.

Then, teach yourself to listen. Truly listen. You'll become skilled in the art if you'll *concentrate on what the speaker is saying* instead of trying to formulate your answer. You can't do both. Make your comments and any questions relate to what the speaker actually said.

You can judge your listening by envisioning a conversational pie. If two of you are engaged in a conversation, your share of talk time is roughly 50 percent. Take more only if urged.

Notice how your share becomes smaller as the group becomes larger.

If three of you are involved in a conversation, your share is roughly 33 percent. Take more *only* if urged.

CONVERSATIONAL PIES

 Your share when two of you are talking.

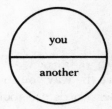 Your share when three of you are talking.

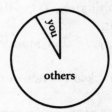 Your share when four of you are talking.

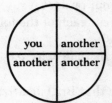 You in a crowd.

If four of you are involved in a conversation, your share is roughly 25 percent. Take more *only* if urged.

If you were dividing the kind of pie you eat, you wouldn't grab the whole thing unless no one else wanted it. The same rules apply here.

Words Are Tools of the Brain

The second dramatic way to improve the way you sound is to pay attention to the words you use. Words are tools of the brain. You blunt those tools at your peril.

Those who would succeed are often in the "public ear." If you are asked to speak before others, you may be jarring more eardrums than you realize.

Take the following word quiz to see if you come across as "lower class" or as a "linguistic cripple."

Read each sentence carefully and indicate what's wrong with it. Does it contain an error in grammar or does it reveal a lack of awareness? How would you express each of the following?

1. After just one week in Hawaii, she was eager to be stateside again.

2. Paul couldn't help but observe that British citizens have a high regard for tiny Prince William.

3. When the Smiths visited Washington, D.C., their first stop was at the Smithsonian Institute.

4. When she visited Texas, she noticed that many workers were digging oil wells.

5. The announcer said, "Reggie Jackson is not in the line-up today; he has a temperature."

6. I am adverse to correcting other people's speech.

7. Her husband went to a specialist to see if he needed treatment for his prostrate gland.

8. The minister insisted on selecting the offeratory.

9. She wrote to the personnel director in regards to her interest in the human resources field.

10. He said that swimming was his forte. (Should he make the word *forte* one syllable or two?)

11. He congratulated the young woman on her engagement.

12. Ever since he took his first course in accounting, he knew he wanted to work for J.C. Penny.

13. He was shocked that his friend, who owned a realty firm, would refuse to sponsor him when he took the relator's test.

14. The suggestion from Joe and myself never made it to the boss.

15. I would of mentioned this sooner if I'd known about it.

16. We better study grammar now if we want to be promoted.

17. Irregardless of what you say, a low-pitched, well-modulated voice will make you seem more impressive.

18. I snuck in a side door so I was not noticed.

19. We finished the meal with sherbert and coffee.

20. It was the heighth of embarrassment to be told that I need to improve my vocabulary.

Bonus Question: What's wrong with this statement?

Sandra O'Day might one day become Chief Justice of the Supreme Court.

ANSWERS TO THE WORD QUIZ

Compare your answers with those shown. Do your answers reveal a lack of awareness or contain errors in grammar? Score yourself and then see how you rate in this important aspect of all work.

1. Hawaii is a state. Hawaiians do not appreciate your excluding them as you do when you say "stateside." Say *mainland* instead.

2. Say British *subjects*. Monarchy, you see.

3. The correct name of the museum is the Smithsonian *Institution*.

4. Texans will remind you that you *drill* for oil.

5. Everyone has a temperature and most of the time it's normal. I believe the announcer meant to say that Reggie Jackson had a *fever*.

6. *Averse* is the word I should have used here. Adverse means detrimental in design or effect: The use of poor grammar causes an adverse reaction. Averse means strongly disinclined.

7. I believe her husband meant to say *prostate* (only one *r* in this word).

8. The word is *offertory*, not offeratory.

9. She wrote in *regard* (no *s* on the end of the word) to her interest.

10. When used in this sense the word is pronounced as though it were *fort* (one syllable).

11. It is considered a breach of etiquette to congratulate the bride or bride-to-be. Congratulations are extended to the bridegroom or bridegroom-to-be and good wishes to the woman. One may congratulate the happy couple.

12. Penney, as in J.C. Penney, is spelled Penney. Job seekers take note.

13. This sentence is included because the president of a realty firm told me he refused to sponsor a friend because the friend persisted in pronouncing realtor as though it were *re-la-tor*. Notice that the first part of the word is *real*, not *re-la*.

14. The sentence should read "The suggestion from Joe and *me*."

15. The sentence should read "I would *have. . .* "

16. The sentence should read "We *had* better. . ."

17. *Irregardless* is not an acceptable word in standard English. The word you want is *regardless*.

18. Say "I *sneaked* in. . . "

19. The preferred spelling and pronunciation: sherb*et* (no second *r*).

20. The word is *height*. It ends with *ht*, not *th*. It rhymes with *right*.

Bonus Question: Sandra Day O'Connor might become Chief Justice of the United States. Note both her name and the title.

Scoring
Start with 100 points. Deduct 5 points for each incorrect answer. Give yourself 5 extra points if you got both parts of the bonus question.

Rate Yourself

90–105   You are an astute person. Your awareness and your command of words make you an obvious candidate for a top spot.

80–85   You are above average.

70–75   You will have to improve your ability to communicate or promotion will be denied you.

60–65   Others often cringe when you speak.

50–55   You will need to eliminate "wince words" from your vocabulary if you expect to move ahead. Your lack of word power may be jeopardizing your present job.

Under 50   Begin immediately to improve your speech. Make columns by Peter Funk, William Safire, and James J. Kilpatrick a part of your reading fare. You can also find help in my book *Word*

Watcher's Handbook: A Deletionary of the Most Abused and Misused Words. It's available for $4.95 plus $1.00 postage and handling from the publisher, St. Martin's Press, 175 Fifth Avenue, New York, N.Y. 10010.

Telephoning

Before I leave this section on sound, I must comment on the use of the telephone.

Telephoning and its impact on your image could be the subject of a complete book. Telephone companies do a fine job on this subject and they will send their material to you free of charge. Ask for a booklet and then study it as though you'd never seen a phone before.

I do have these suggestions:

• Plan your call. Know what you hope to accomplish and how you expect to accomplish it before you dial.

• Have pertinent materials nearby. Anchor pencil and paper to the telephone if necessary. Anticipate requests for information and be ready with your calendar and appropriate files.

• Prepare and rehearse your opening statement if the call is an important one.

• Clearly identify yourself and your firm, and state the purpose of your call.

• Speak directly into the mouthpiece. Never smoke, eat, or chew gum while telephoning.

• Don't breathe into the phone. This is audible at the other end.

• If you are calling from a phone booth or other noisy place, cover the mouthpiece with your hand while the other person is speaking.

• Use a tape recorder and tape yourself as you use the telephone. Do this for at least a week. Then listen to the way you come across. Also, have someone whose opinion you respect listen to your tapes and critique your telephone image. Ask your monitor to pay particular attention to errors in grammar you might make and to tell you about tiresome phrases you use. No, you won't notice them. We screen our own mistakes. (Do not tape another person without permission.)

Those Dratted Message Machines

I thought all of us came across poorly on these until I had my first message from my friend Carole Wilson. Her message went something like this:

> "Phyllis dear, This is Carole Wilson trying to reach you on Thursday afternoon. If you can join me for lunch next Tuesday to discuss Advocate Awards, let me know by Monday noon. My number is 100–1000. Let me repeat that number. It is 100–1000. 'Bye."

Since then, I've resolved to write down all phone messages I want to deliver *before* my dial finger gets busy.

In preparing my message, I follow Carole's example. I include:

- my name
- purpose of call
- time of call
- whether or not I expect a return call
- my phone number, twice

Carole's message not only covered all of the above but also set a time frame for all the other calls that were on the machine with hers.

Note: Don't get cute with your message. This is annoying and it does not do anything for your image.

Phone Tips for Your Secretary

• Never have him or her say, "Barbara's still out to lunch," or worse still, "Jim hasn't come in yet." A simple "Ms. Smith is not in at the moment" will do.

• If you need to screen calls, have your secretary say, "One moment, let me see if she's available. May I tell her who's calling?" Don't have your secretary pull that business about "I'll see if she's in." A good secretary knows damned well whether you're at work.

• Have your secretary say when answering the phone, "Barbara Smith's office, June Holden speaking." Then when turning the phone over to you, the secretary addresses you as Ms., Miss, Mrs., or Dr., giving you the preferred designation.

You will, of course, give your secretary and someone else's secretary the respect that person deserves. Treat the secretary as an intelligent adult and give messages when appropriate. Many times the secretary can solve the problem and this makes everybody look good.

Special Courtesies

• Return phone calls. Mature men and women return calls, even when doing so isn't pleasant. Postponing a call doesn't make it any easier.

• Be especially conscious of time when someone calls you long distance. It's the caller's money, so don't take advantage by dragging out the conversation with unrelated topics.

• Be extremely careful about the messages you take for others. You need all of the following information:
> for whom intended
> the exact time the message was received
> your name or initials
> the message itself
> from whom the message was received (the full name, including the correct designation of Mr., Dr., Miss, Ms., or Mrs.). This helps the recipient appear smarter when answering the message.

Every item is important. Yes, even to putting down the exact time of the call. At times the person for whom the message is intended will have encountered the person who called and transacted the necessary business on the way back to his or her desk. The exact time reveals whether the message concerns new business or refers to the business already handled.

THE SENSE OF TOUCH

If we use good sense about our sense of touch, touching can be our most effective means of communicating.

For a while those who were trying to "get in touch" with their feelings brought out the touchiness in others who were uncomfortable with all the raised consciousness and touching going on.

No matter how much in touch with ourselves we may be, we have to acknowledge that some people do not want us to be "in touch" with them if it means touching them physically. Everyone has to have a certain amount of personal space, and we don't invade another's space or territory without invitation. It's smart to find out how much personal space each colleague needs. The variance is great.

Knowing when and when not to touch extends beyond touching another person. We do not touch another's possessions unless we're sure that touch is welcome. A clue: When it's referred to as fingering, you will know that the touching is unwelcome.

Let me cite an example of fingering or the unwelcome touch. I saw a fellow worker enter a colleague's office and pick up a monogrammed calendar from the desk and remark on it. After the visiting employee left, the man whose office had been invaded took out a tissue and without a word carefully wiped off the calendar.

Welcome Touches

A Pat on the Back
This is almost always in order as a way of saying, "Good job" or "Congratulations."

The Handshake
Your handshake should be healthy and confident, firm, but never hurtful to the other person. Certainly never flabby. Negative handshakes have often been described as "limp fish" or "bone crushers."

In order to deliver a confident handshake, you'll need to think about it ahead of time. When you are in a situation that could call for a handshake, be ready by transferring your briefcase or glasses to your left hand. Also, try to keep your hand warm. Many thoughtful ones learn to hold a drink with the left hand or to wrap a napkin around the cold glass so the recipient of the handshake doesn't feel cold flesh.

When do you shake hands?

- Always when a hand is offered
- Usually when you introduce yourself or are introduced to someone
- Often if you encounter a colleague when you are away from your place of employment
- When you reach an agreement with someone
- When you end a professional encounter

The Embrace
Nothing is so expressive as the embrace as a way of expressing sympathy. Words can be misunderstood; the *friendly* embrace seldom. Embracing at other times should probably occur in another place, rather than in a business office. You'll have to judge those situations by awareness of what could and could not be construed as sexual harassment.

Before we leave the subject of touching, I'd like to suggest that you read Ashley Montagu's splendid book on the subject. It's called *Touching*. What else?

THE SWEET SMELL OF SUCCESS

As I typed the word *smell* I could remember the aroma of Mother's newly baked bread. Makes me want to get out the flour, search for some yeast, bring the milk to almost scalding, knead a bit, and then await the savory result.

My nose also remembers the fragrance of bed linen after it had dried outdoors. Did you ever do what I used to do: actually bury your face in the pillowcase and breathe deeply in order to drink in the smell?

I hope you did, for the smell of success is something like that: clean, fresh, sweet, seductive as all get-out.

Why am I talking about the sweet *smell* of success? Because the effectiveness of the fresh, clean smell has been overlooked, underrated, unrecognized, unremarked but never, never underpowered. It is *potent*.

If you don't go along with the truth of this, breathe deeply when you are around the great ones. The aura—the aroma of success—is intertwined with the scent of cleanliness. It surrounds the great ones and is almost palpable.

No halitosis or—forgive the expression—"body odor" is in the air. And, my dears, it *is* in the air with some of the losers. You didn't ask but I'll tell you: One of the most distasteful tasks of personnel people is to tell the offenders they offend. Yes, I've had to do it.

While the "By the way, your deodorant is letting you down" interview is *not* easy, it's surprisingly effective. After the problem is "aired," the offender no longer offends. Not for a while anyway. Even those with dental and medical problems usually find solutions.

And still on the subject of scents, let me mention the commercial kind: perfume, cologne, after-shave lotion. If they are *below* the conscious awareness of colleagues and if they are worn on clean bodies, the effect produced is usually positive.

TASTE: IT'S NOT ALL IN YOUR MOUTH

The kind of taste I'm talking about usually has the word *good* in front of it.

Because nobody else is stepping forward at the moment, I'll offer my definition: Good taste embodies manners, breeding, and consideration—all those qualities that make human interaction more pleasant.

The sense of taste interacts with all the other senses we've been talking about.

Good taste is the quality that is reflected in your choice of what you wear, what you say, and what possessions you choose to have around you. Those with good taste don't impinge on another's time or territory without invitation or assurance of welcome. Nor does the possessor of good taste issue invitations that the invitee has difficulty refusing. Invitations that are issued too far in advance or that force the recipient to select a time are shows of rudeness, not courtesy.

Good taste—or if you prefer, style—can be heightened by paying attention to many little details that can make a big difference. Let's get downright picky about some of those details.

Picky, Picky, Picky

Your Business Card
Its appearance reflects your taste or lack of it. If you or your company cannot spring for quality paper and quality printing, forget the business card.

A good test of whether your card is too busy is this one: Your card should have enough clear space so that you can place a quarter on it without the quarter's touching print. You can forget the cutesy logos or background pictures (unless you work for Kodak—the photos on their cards are extremely well done).

Avoid too many type sizes and faces. Good color choices for the card are white, cream, or gray. Contrasting ink should be confined to one color, two at most. Embossed or raised lettering is considered to be in good taste. The "parchment" look is tacky.

Stationery

Your personal letter paper is an extension and a reflection of you. Be sure it is of quality bond and that you have matching envelopes. Monarch size is very popular with executives.

Whether your secretary types your business letters or you do, there should be no typos, no misspellings, no whiteout blotches. The letters should allow for wide margins and those margins should be even.

And need I say?—no erasable bond. Ever.

About the Color of Ink You Use

Black is considered the executive's color. You might make an exception when you are sending form letters; a signature in blue ink will show that the letter was individually signed.

If your handwriting is not legible, be sure your name is typed below your signature. And, please, no unnecessary affectations or flourishes. I've lost count of the negative comments I've heard about circles for dots over *i*'s and other airs.

About Sending Copies

This tip will cost you an extra minute or two but it's time well spent. Arrange the names of those receiving copies with the recipient's name at the top of the list. For instance, if you don't know who is the more important, Mr. Brown or Ms. Smith, don't just blithely list them in alphabetical order. On Ms. Smith's copy, let her name appear first; and on Mr. Brown's copy, his name is mentioned first.

Why?

For one thing, people have a greater tendency to read copies of anything when their name is high on the list of recipients. For another, this is a chance to rub someone the right way. If Ms. Smith thinks she is more important to you than is Mr. Brown, she may respond positively to your message and to you.

If the chairman of the board and the president are receiving copies, their names head any list. You'd look like a dodo if you tampered with that.

Instead of putting "cc" (stands for carbon copy) at the bottom of your letter, put "copy to." Fewer people are using carbon these days. With this newer version, you'll seem more up-to-the-minute even if your equipment isn't.

Clippings

The way you clip clippings reveals whether you're newsworthy yourself. The knowledgeable person is careful to include the *name of the newspaper* and the *date*; otherwise the clipping is almost useless. The poor impression you leave when you send an undated clipping from heaven-knows-what publication is needlessly damaging. Worse still, you've blown a chance to show the newsworthy one that you're informed as well as thoughtful.

What Does Your Office Say about You?

You might not have a "say" in the selection of office furniture. But you do have a measure of control over the visual attractiveness of your office and the message it conveys about your efficiency.

The person with taste will select accoutrements with consideration for the message those items convey. Your investment in quality items could give you good return on that investment.

The Person With Taste	**The Tacky Person**
• chooses items of durable materials such as leather, wood, and quality glass (such as Orrefors)	• likes plastic, fake leather
• selects a functional calendar of simple design	• selects a calendar decorated with questionable pictures *(Playgirl/Playboy)* or one with questionable jokes of the day, week, month
• selects an easy-to-read clock that serves the visitor as well as the occupant	• prefers a clock of flashy design, which announces the time at regular intervals by a catchy ding-dong or tune
• keeps a desk pen handy (and operable) for visitor's use	• can't even find his or her own pen
• selects paintings in keeping with the decor of the office	• covers the wall with trendy slogans or unframed posters
• even when confronted with numerous papers and material for a project, aligns those papers in neat stacks	• has papers and files strewn all over the office to demonstrate busyness

When/if you can control it, ask for the corner office or the one with a window—preferably one close to the person with the most power. Often, if you have a lot to discuss with that person, such a move can seem a logical one.

I still chuckle as I remember one young rising star who actually acquired an office by moving his papers into an empty one. "Needed the privacy," he said, because of the confidential nature of the report he was working on. You might try this too. A legitimate reason to request privacy— i.e. your own office—would be to conduct sensitive interviews. If you discuss jobs, money, benefits, or other confidential matters, consider asking for the proper place in which to do it.

Eating with Taste

If dining out with your employer—or a prospective employer—is inevitable, vow to carry it off with style. You can if you think about it ahead of time; in fact, you can even decide what to order. Or come close to it, anyway.

For example, a little forethought will keep you from ordering lobster, soup containing cheese that is stringy, or something such as artichoke. Forethought will suggest grapefruit juice over grapefruit. Remember to order food that is simple to eat and that does not make you look awkward. Also remember when the rolls are served that soft ones don't leave all those crumbs on the table as hard ones do.

It is not necessary to take a drink if one is offered. If you want one and know how to handle it, follow your preference. I would strongly advise against your taking more than one. If you don't want one, simply order juice or mineral water. That way you won't seem to be telling your host what to do or not to do.

A reader of my job column told me that his recruiter handed him the wine list and asked him to make the selection. The candidate was completely befuddled because he couldn't even pronounce the names, let alone select a suitable wine. If this happens to you, you can always say, "I'm sure you have a favorite. Shall we order that?"

Other tips for reducing the tension in a possibly high-tension situation would be these:

• Take smaller bites than usual.

• As always, cut one piece of meat at a time, but make the pieces a bit smaller than usual.

• Refrain from mashing your food.

• Do not talk with your mouth full. You may nod to acknowledge that you heard a question but wait until you have swallowed your food before answering.

• Do not season the food *before* tasting it. This is an insult to the chef and it did, in fact, cost a candidate a job. The propsective employer decided the candidate would make decisions before checking the facts.

• Never use your finger to push food onto your fork.

• Use your utensils by starting with the first fork or spoon on the outside of the setting and using each consecutive piece of flatware as each course is served.

• Never say, "I'm full" or push your plate away. Stacking dishes and clearing the table is not the responsibility of the diner. One young employee's wife created a poor impression by handing her dishes to the back waiter (busboy).

• Never say, "I'm done" or even "I'm finished." Announce this fact by silent signals, or else you may be finished altogether. Simply put your knife and fork in a parallel position on your plate to indicate you've finished with them.

Your host will probably also do this. Wait until he or she has placed the napkin on the table at the end of the meal, then do the same. This will signal the end of the meal.

I use the book *Executive Etiquette* as a reference (see Bibliography). I urge you to do the same.

Part II
SELF-MODIFICATION

3

DEVELOPING THE

PROFESSIONAL PROFILE

This chapter is designed to help you determine and develop your professional potential. By examining your own attitudes, standards, and behaviors, you'll be able to measure the perceptions others have of you.

Are you seen as one who is outstandingly competent in your particular field or occupation?

After taking the following test you'll be able to answer this basic question with accuracy. What's more, you'll have a clear idea of where you might fall short of the mark.

Ideally, you should devote one week to studying this chapter.

Take the test, answering every *appropriate* question, score it carefully, and make a list of areas that need your attention. It helps to say to yourself: I will make a commitment to improve this aspect of my work life and I will put forth an extra effort until habit takes over and the new behavior is part of me.

ABOUT THE TEST

It's presumptuous to make up a test such as the one that follows. And, of course, many of you will take issue with the point value assigned to each question.

47

Good.

I argued with myself about it, too. For example, I was particularly uncomfortable with deducting a whopping 16 points (number 39) because a person was passed over for promotion three times. But—after a lot of juggling—I knew I had to do so.

Top management rarely overlooks an employee with true potential. But once they do, it becomes easier to do it a second time. And when it's time for a third look, the look is a fleeting one. The reasoning seems to be: We, the "all knowing," wouldn't have passed over someone with true promise so there must be something wrong with so-and-so. Consequently, the 16-point penalty must stand.

Number 21 bothers me, too. I know that lying could cost a job rather than the mere 2 points I charge the culprit. But if the test taker is still on the premises I must assume the "cost" is being charged to the account for the time being. Actually, *any* one of the factors covered could make, or break, a career.

I changed the quiz itself more times than I can count. At first, I included a question about alcohol abuse; that question generated one about illegal use of drugs. While I wrestled with these issues a bright colleague remarked that "boozers" and those who "do drugs" will not consider *their* use excessive. To include such questions would skew the scoring. What's more, those issues *are* covered by other questions. When work is impaired, raises and promotions withheld (issues addressed in other questions), drugs, both legal and illegal, are often contributing factors. I did consider these and other factors that don't leap out at you as you take the test.

While this is a simple test, it has real substance—a substance born of experience. I approached the construction of this test very seriously; I hope you consider your answers very seriously. Taking the test won't solve your problems (if any), but it will alert you to them.

This test has been given to men and women in a variety of fields including marketing, manufacturing, education, government, finance, and social service. Test takers range from the less-than-successful secretary up to the chief executive officer.

Each test taker has learned that everyone has areas of inadequacy. And the smart ones are taking responsibility for the development of a stronger professional profile.

DEVELOPING THE PROFESSIONAL PROFILE

Scaling the Heights

Use the following scale to draw your own success profile.

Please answer questions that apply to *your* situation; not all questions are pertinent for every test taker. You should manage to answer thirty-five of the forty-two questions listed.

	Yes +	No −

1. Have you trained a successor? If self-employed, do you have a reliable person to represent your interests when you're unavailable? A yes answer is worth 5 points.

2. Do you make a consistent effort to get the best talent around you? If yes, add 2 points to your score.

3. Are you persistent? Can you stay on track regardless of obstacles? If yes, add 2 points.

4. Note: If visibility is regarded as a negative in your organization, please skip part B of this question.

   Are you visible? A. Are you known to the president of your organization? If yes, give yourself 2 points. B. Does the local newspa-

	Yes	No
	+	−

per have a file on you? If yes, give yourself another 2 points.

5. Do you have vision? Can you paint a clear picture of the desired work objective? Is that picture clear enough so that those with whom you work are inspired by it? If yes, give yourself 3 points.

6. Have you the ability to adapt to the terrain? Do the words *resilient* and *flexible* describe you? A yes is worth 2 points.

7. Do you feel as though you own the place; i.e., do you take responsibility for what goes on? Do you refer to your organization as *we* or *they?* If you answered *we*, give yourself 2 points.

8. How involved are you in promoting your boss? Can you—right now—name five responsibilities that fall to your boss? Give yourself a point for each responsibility you name.

9. Do you take responsibility for your own career path? If yes, give yourself 3 points.

10. A. How do you rate as a speaker? If above average, give yourself 3 points. B. How did you score on the word awareness test in Chapter 2? If above 90, give yourself a pat on the back and add another 3 points in the yes column; if 70–80 there is no point value; if you scored below 70, put 5 points in the no

	Yes	No
	+	−

column and begin a serious study of word usage.

11. Are you asked to handle correspondence and important written material for others? If so, give yourself 3 points.

12. How much do you read? Do you subscribe to newspapers in addition to your local paper? Business magazines? Give yourself a point for each publication (over and above your local newspaper) that you *read* regularly.

13. How is your appearance? Excellent—5 points. Above average—2 points. Average— no points. Not quite up to the mark—deduct 5 points.

14. How extensive is your grasp of the new technology? If better than average, give yourself 4 points. If average, there is no point value. If you're a true technophobe and you're not doing anything about it, deduct 5 points.

15. Do you live in the same area of town as those on your top management team? Belong to the same club(s)? Have mutual friends? Each yes answer is worth 2 points. (If you're self-employed, these questions pertain to those persons whose decisions affect your career.)

16. Have you a touch of audacity? Do you ask for what you want? Would you nominate yourself for office if no one else did and you felt

	Yes	No
	+	−

yourself qualified? Would you ask to be considered for a position two rungs up the ladder from your present one if you had the proper qualifications? If you answer yes to one or more of the above, give yourself 5 points.

17. How effective are you at saying no? Very—4 points. Average—1 point. If saying no is difficult for you, deduct 4 points.

18. Is your desire to get things done stronger than your desire to be liked? Yes—3 points. No—subtract 4 points.

19. Do you have control over how most of your work time is spent? If yes, give yourself 4 points. If no, subtract 2 points.

20. How is your energy level? If you're above average—2 points. None for average or below.

21. Have you an ethical compass? If yes, give yourself 2 points. Would you lie, if necessary, in order to advance in your work? If yes, take away your 2 points. Have you ever taken credit for another's work? If yes, deduct 6 points.

22. Has an executive recruiter tried to hire you? Within the last year?—add 2 points. Within the last two or three years?—add 1 point. No, never—deduct 5 points.

	Yes	No
	+	−

23. Do you know how government affects your business? Are grants involved? What laws affect the operation of your business? What enforcement agencies dictate policy? If you can answer *all* of these questions, add 5 points. If you are uninformed about *any* of the questions, deduct 3 points.

24. Are you considered a delegator? Yes—4 points. If no, deduct 3 points.

25. Professional organizations:

Are you fairly active? Have you held high office (president or board level)? Yes—2 points.

Are you usually the organizational workhorse? Yes—no points.

Do you belong to professional societies? If no involvement, deduct 1 point.

26. Which word best describes you?
Plotter? Deduct 2 points.
Plodder? Deduct 3 points.
Planner? Add 5 points.

27. Have you documented your training? Have you the appropriate degree for your work? Yes—add 5 points.

Have you acquired additional training and education since employment? Yes—add 4 points.

Have you acquired valuable practical experience? Yes—add 4 points.

	Yes	No
	+	−

28. If your organization is international in scope, have you had an overseas assignment or responsibility for foreign operations? If yes, add 5 points.

29. Are you willing to take risks and to pay the price for having taken them? If so, add 3 points.

30. Do you have the ability to organize your work? The work of those who report to you? Give yourself 2 points for each yes answer.

31. How do others describe your attitude? Positive—add 5 points. Negative—deduct 5 points. Average—no point value.

32. Do you document—put in writing—your best ideas? If yes, add 2 points.

33. Have you good access to information about your organization or field of work? Yes—4 points.

34. It's not enough to work like a dog; are you willing to tackle the "dog" jobs? Add 2 points for a yes answer.

35. Do you know what you want—what gives you job satisfaction? Give yourself 3 points if you could, or did, put this answer into words.

36. Have you had a salary increase within the last 6 months that exceeds what the cost-of-living index would suggest? If so, add 2 points.

	Yes	No
	+	−

Have you had two such increases within the last 18 months? If so, add another 5 points.

If self-employed, has your income risen more than 12 percent in the last 6 months? If so, add 2 points. If your income has increased by more than 25 percent in the past 18 months, add another 5 points.

37. If you have a set of advisers—what amounts to your own board of directors—from business and academe, give yourself 5 points.

If you have a sponsor, godmother/godfather, mentor, or angel within your organization or field of work, give yourself 2 points.

(Yes answers can add up to a total of 7 points.)

38. Do you have a strong support system? From above—2 points. Lateral support—2 points. From below—2 points. If you enjoy support from *all* three categories, give yourself a total of 8 points for this question.

39. Have you been passed over for promotion? If once, deduct 2 points. If twice, deduct 5 points. If passed over three times, deduct 16 points.

40. Are you in the same field of work as those on your top management team? For example, if they are in marketing and you are too, add 4 points to your score. If no one in your field has reached the top level of management, deduct 3 points.

	Yes	No
	+	−

41. Do you keep your boss informed? If yes, give yourself 3 points. If you keep your boss informed about positives *in writing*, give yourself an extra 2 points. If you tell your boss about negatives *in writing*, deduct 2 points.

42. Can you read organizational signals? Can you assess any discrepancy between what the organization *says* it wants and what is actually valued and rewarded? Yes—3 points. No—deduct 2 points.

Scoring

Add all the numbers in the yes column; subtract from this the total of the no answers. The remaining figure is your score.

A score of 90 is average. In order to consider yourself promotable, you should score 100 or better.

If you score above 125 points, promotion is assured. And, if you approach the 165 mark, you're probably a CEO or soon will be.

After scoring the test, take another look at all the questions where you had a minus answer. If there is no appropriate action required from you to bring this to a plus answer, forget it. (Question 40 is an example; you probably will not want to change your field of work simply because your top managers are in another.)

But look at number 23—the opposite is true. If you scored a minus here, action is imperative.

To get full benefit from the test, go back and study *each* of your answers. Strive to change or modify your behavior where such action will help you to become an "anointed one."

PERFORMANCE APPRAISALS

I include here a deceptively simple appraisal form.

The key point I wish to make is this: Everybody who works for anybody is rated. Rarely is the actual rating—or report card—shown to the person being rated. Even CEOs are rated by a board of directors.

I hesitated to use "attendance" and "púnctuality" in a book for you highly educated, sophisticated types. But those factors do have a bearing on your professional profile.

During the course of developing this chapter, I conducted a motivational seminar for bank officials. When I showed this portion to one of the vice presidents, he sniffed audibly as he warned me against a "kindergarten approach" to appraisal. However, *his* boss, the president, praised it; and, during the "attitude adjustment period" before dinner, he asked me to include some remarks about attendance, punctuality, and just being where one is expected to be. "That *%o$%*ß%o [he pointed to the vice president] is never in his office when I look for him."

So, use this form to do your own appraisal on a periodic basis. If you do it well, you won't have to worry about the appraisal someone else is doing on you.

Employee Appraisal Form

PERFORMANCE REPORT

NAME_____PERIOD ENDING_____
POSITION_____ DEPT._____DATE DUE_____

CHECK ( )APPRAISALS

Performance factors

	Unsatis-factory	Improve-ment Needed	Satis-factory	Very Good	Excel-lent
1. Attendance	1				
2. Punctuality	2				
3. Appearance	3				
4. Attitude	4				
5. Potential	5				

Over-all appraisal: should reflect the above information	Unsatis-factory	Improve-ment Needed	Satis-factory	Very Good	Excel-lent

APPRAISER_____

There is often a "departmental rating sheet" that accompanies the individual rating sheet you see here. On these forms, the manager is asked to rank each employee according to value to the team effort or value to the department. For example: When there are 25 employees, the manager would say in essence, "If I could keep only one person (and had to release the others), I would choose _____. If I could keep only two persons, they would be _____ and _____." And so on down to poor old number 25.

Suppose your manager made such a rating, where would you stand? Think about it.

4
MASTERING THE
MARTECHNIQUE
OF TIME MANAGEMENT

*Much may be done in those little shreds and patches of
time, which every day produces, and which most men
throw away.*

—Caleb C. Colton

The Rev. Mr. Colton had a good point there. I'd like to shout
"amen" and then amend what he said. My version: Much has
to be done in those little shreds and patches of time because
those little shreds and patches of time are *all we are going to
have.* Ever.

WHAT TO DO TO MAKE BETTER USE OF YOUR TIME

We must realize that time is not handed to us whole (i.e.
without any demands, obligations, or unfilled promises). We
can vow to make use of those precious tag ends of time.

We know, for example, that a patchwork quilt can be a
lovely thing if the pieces are put together with some sort of
design. The design we fashion with our time can be the goal
we set for ourselves. Goals, really, for our little goals become
a part of our bigger goals.

Time is always on the side of the person with clear-cut
aims.

59

If you haven't already been prodded into asking yourself these questions, do it now:

- What do I want to do?
- Where do I want to go?
- And, most important of all, what do I want to become? To be?

For what you are to be, you are *now* becoming. If you want to be the mayor of your town, the superintendent of schools, tops in sales, the star of your community theater group, or an "anointed one" in your organization, you must make time your ally.

Because time doesn't usually come to us in whole days, weeks, or months, we must reckon with it as it comes: in seconds, minutes, and, if we're lucky, in hours.

Make Time Your Ally

In making time your ally, it's smart to hit "big-ticket" items first. Here are my six best "big-ticket" time tips:

1. *Promise everything later than you can deliver it.* I will credit following that practice with any success I've ever had. Anywhere. It has also given me a great deal of private amusement.

It's so simple, really. You are often asked when a project will be finished because you're the only one who can predict the time accurately. Make the answer realistic. Don't try to please with a promise, only to disappoint later. Here's a list of the results this practice can bring:

- You finish everything ahead of schedule.
- You're regarded as a doer.
- You never put your superiors in a dither about whether you'll come through.

- You're not under pressure and so do better work.
- You can *relax*. If that confounded report isn't due until Wednesday, smile—*you* know you *could* have it ready by Tuesday.
- You make your boss look good. Often his or her report depends on your report.
- An unexpected snag or delay won't throw you.
- You won't have someone staring over your shoulder at deadline time because you've *already beaten the deadline*.

2. *Do your work in the order of its importance.* I know of an instance in which a manager paid a consultant $25,000 for this advice. While the consultant's verbiage was more impressive than mine, this is what he meant. Put the most important project at the top of your list and the least important one at the bottom. And do them in that order.

3. *Learn to say YES to that which you enjoy.* There is a lurking guilt in all of us that says, "I enjoy this; it must not be worthwhile." What nonsense. We perform best the jobs we enjoy. I once counseled a returning homemaker who almost didn't tell me how skilled a bridge player she was because bridge was for "enjoyment." You guessed it. She's now using bridge in her work as a director of tournament play. Often on cruise ships.

You will, of course, take into account the needs of your employer, *from whom all blessings flow.*

A part of this tip is also to cultivate the people you enjoy, both socially and in a business setting. Do this and I promise you, you won't have time left over to be the reluctant companion of bores.

4. *Learn to say NO.* This takes gallantry, guts, and gusto. You're halfway there if you'll rehearse your NO before your performance. Actually write out what you must say *before* you're asked. Quickly now, take pen in hand and compose your response to the next unmanageable request.

Borrow these if need be:

- "If you must have an immediate answer, it will have to be no."
- "I agree, your project is worthwhile. But so are the three to which I'm already committed."
- "How flattering for you to think of me. Sorry I can't manage it."

Because I write at home—and because I don't write at all on the days I yield to the temptation of lunch with friends—I've committed this ditty to memory. When cornered to "name a time," I recite the

Editor's Lament

Thanks a bunch,
But don't take my writer to lunch.
Though you're willing to pay,
It costs her a day.
Don't take my writer to lunch.

5. *Structure your work.* If your job requires you to grant interviews, schedule them during specific hours. If you must be flexible, be flexible one day each week, not *every* day.

Incoming mail and dictation should be handled at the same time. Try to react to mail only once. Master the art of tossing, answering, or referring mail as you receive it. If your mental style requires a digestion period, at least sort your mail. In sorting, be sure that trash hits the trash basket immediately.

Initiate necessary phone calls and make them when you can group them. When someone must call you, a tactful "I'm easy to reach between 8:30 and 10:00 A.M." gets the idea across. You can produce efficiency in your caller by giving a warm "Hello, So-and-So" followed by "And what can I do for you today?" or "How can I help you?" Your friendly offer forces the caller to state the purpose of the call immediately.

Know how much time each project is worth and budget the time allotted to it.

6. *Let George do it.* Learn to delegate.

Delegating assignments is not only an effective time-saver, it's an effective way to train your successor so the transition will be smooth when you're promoted. You and I both know, you can't move up if your promotion will "cause waves" where you are now.

Be creative about delegating. You can even delegate reading material; such delegation broadens your outlook as well as that of your subordinate.

And, of course, you'll delegate a part of your correspondence, both incoming and outgoing. No need for you to see all the incoming junk mail and no need for *you* to see letters a trusted secretary or assistant can handle.

You can also assign portions of reports for which you're responsible. Naturally, you will give credit to the person who did the actual work on a particular segment. And you will, I hope, explain the purpose and scope of the project as well as giving the expected time commitment.

Warning note: One can carry this delegating too far. I well remember remarking to my assistant as I left town one day, "Whew, I've finally gotten everything off my calendar." "Yes," she replied, "and onto mine."

"Little-Ticket" Time Tips

• Make a travel list of items you need for every trip and place a copy in *each* travel bag. I can almost pack without conscious thought as I look at mine: contact lens gear, curling iron, blow dryer, cosmetic kit, bedroom slippers, names of local media people, ticket, schedule, etc.

• If your work is segmented or compartmentalized, have different briefcases in which the files are kept. For example, I know of a school supervisor who visits fourteen schools. She has a briefcase for each.

• Order all tickets through your travel agent. They're very good at saving your money and your time. And they provide a schedule. *Knowing* you'll be served a meal or a snack on a given flight can save you half an hour or so on a busy day.

• If you're forced to reschedule a flight while en route, do not get in that long line with all your fellow passengers who are also trying to reschedule. Simply trot to the nearest phone booth and call your travel agent, the airline that bumped you, or the most logical carrier and arrange for the next flight out of there. I am indebted to Leland Davis, time-management consultant, for this one. Thanks, Leland, you've saved me countless hours.

• Never enter a waiting room empty-handed. Carry stamped, addressed envelopes and letter paper with you. Any correspondence that can be handwritten can be handled in this time slot. This can also be a productive time for making outlines, lists of projects, and for catching up on reading that would put you to sleep in a more congenial situation.

• When colleagues ask to confer with you, try to meet in their offices instead of yours. It's much easier to leave than to get someone else to.

• If you are to meet with someone whose office is not close to yours, try to meet at your place. That way, you save the travel time.

• Keep a telephone timer on hand. This is a good reminder to you and your caller to confine the call to the business at hand.

THE ENEMIES OF TIME

Learn to recognize the enemies of time:

• *Lost items.* Surveys on "unproductive time" agree that *looking for lost items* is the greatest of all time wasters. Force yourself to develop an effective filing and labeling system. And do have a special place for important keys and for your glasses.

Never put a paper clip on material that goes into a file drawer. The piece of paper you most want will attach itself behind something you're obviously not seeking.

• *Unnecessary meetings and meetings that are unnecessarily long.* Set a time limit for meetings and have a written agenda. If you must attend a meeting controlled by another person, find out what is expected of you and for how long.

• *Poor timing.* We often feel a necessity to compensate by spending more time on a project because we weren't timely with it. Timeliness is also a factor in producing better results.

• *Procrastination* is an enemy of time. To help myself out of the procrastination trap, I say, "Tomorrow is a vamp." Meaning, of course, that the word *tomorrow* is as seductive as all get-out. Having said this to myself, I then start doing whatever it is I'm supposed to be doing.

• *"Sometime"* is an enemy of time.

• *Excusing our inaction* is an enemy of time.

• *Regretting* is an enemy of time. Let whatever was in the past stay there and look forward instead.

• *Failing to recognize that you're in the prime time of life.* Once you convince yourself of this, your employer (or prospective employer) will also be convinced.

• *Worry is a great enemy of time.* It robs us of energy as well as time. There is a way out of the worry trap. Plan your worrying and set a specific time for it. If you do, the rest of your time is free for creative, constructive action.

Be a "Wednesday worrier."

My mother taught me this one. The system is very simple. You set aside some time every Wednesday for worry. Wednesday worrying has several advantages. Wednesday worrying doesn't interfere with your weekend, your celebration of Friday, or getting into gear on Monday.

If you will actually put on your calendar the items you intend to worry about, you will no longer be burdened with having them play over and over in your mind. Furthermore, a good many worries will disappear by the time your worry day arrives.

Deliberately worrying on one day saves you six whole days of worry time.

All right, I'll admit I hope you had a chuckle when you read about "Wednesday worrying," but let me assure you it works. I laughed too when my mother suggested it the first time. After a while I gave in and tried it. It works so well I'd feel guilty not telling you about it. I recommend it. Wholeheartedly. And very seriously.

Finally, recognize that your time has a dollar value. Treat it as though you are actually ascribing this dollar value to the minutes, hours, and days. Successful consultants do this and it is what you must do if you expect to move forward and upward.

Only when you treat your time with respect will others have high regard for it.

5

MAKING WOE

WORK FOR YOU

There's little point in my writing a book on how to be a winner unless I also discuss how to lose.

Losers can't become winners until they learn the basics of losing. Winners—real winners—know there is a flip side to failure. And they use it. Oh, how they use it. Every rejection, every failure, is used as a tool to forge victory.

Ever notice how seriously a football team goes over the game films? Not just to exult over the sparkling plays but to study every fumble, every missed tackle, and every penalty in order to turn those mistakes into winning plays the next time.

The purpose of this chapter is to turn your losing plays into winning ones; it is to help you recover from being down on yourself after a fumble or what you perceive as a failure or a rejection. And to make woe work *for* you.

Suppose you didn't close that big sale? Suppose you weren't offered the job you were seeking or the promotion you worked for? Suppose you've had it with your job and must quit? Or, suppose you've been fired or might be?

Nobody wins 'em all. But there is a big difference between winners and losers in the way they respond to trouble.

FIVE RULES FOR MANAGING REJECTION

To get the hang of using rejection as a tool, consider these five rules for managing rejection. With five rules, you have one for every working day; start by devoting one full day to the study and implementation of each. They'll soon become ingrained.

1. Expect Rejection.

It happens to everybody, even the great ones. Perhaps mainly to the great ones because the great ones try harder and more often. What's more, they don't quit after a setback.

Babe Ruth held numerous batting records during his lifetime. You'll remember him best for his phenomenal record as a home-run hitter.

But what of his record for strikeouts? Did you know he struck out more than any player in history? Yes, 1,330 times.

And did you know that *Punch* magazine rejected material from—of all people—Charles Dickens? And that Frederick Forsyth's best-best-selling *The Day of the Jackal* was turned down with this comment, "No reader interest"? It has since sold eight million copies.

When you expect rejection—actually prepare for it—you minimize the stress that accompanies it. For stress is the result of not knowing what to do. If you can describe and dissect the experience, you can figure out whether your reaction is intensified by a tie to a previous anxiety. This is a positive approach in recovering from your misery and in discovering how to prepare for the next rejection.

Randy Sher, who is a career consultant based in Detroit, prepares her job seekers this way. She asks them to save all their rejections and take them to the next job seminar. Each job seeker "antes up" and the rejections are thrown into a pot.

The winner?

The one with the most rejections, of course. Need I tell you the one who garners the most rejections is almost always the winner of the next job offer?

Expect rejection, have your plan for dealing with it ready, and persist in your undertaking if you would win. Failure is, as they say, "The line of least persistence."

2. Revel in the Raw Power that Rejection Generates.
Rejection often results in rage and rage is raw power. It's possible you will have more raw power on tap immediately after a rejection than at any other time.

Many people will try to contain such fury, others will give vent to their rage by directing it toward the person who snubbed or rejected them. And a few will release it as positive energy.

Rejection-generated rage can make fools or felons out of the best of us. Lawyer and author Charles J. Guiteau ruined his life and ended that of President James A. Garfield because of rejection. Guiteau was enraged because the president hadn't named him ambassador to Spain.

Today's newspaper will provide more recent examples of this emotion that kills. But for you there's a better way.

If you will internalize rule number one, that of expecting rejection, you will be prepared for step number two, which is to revel in the raw power generated by rejection.

Prepare to let this high level of energy motivate you. If you're passed over for promotion, activate your plan to groom yourself for a better job—inside or outside your present organization. If a publisher rejects your offering, strengthen it and send it to a bigger and better house. If a friend fails you, broaden yourself and your circle by making new friends.

The period after rejection is a time for action. You have a choice about how to act; make the best of it or make the worst of it.

3. Don't Let Rejection Spread From One Area of Your Life to Another.

One rejection can make you feel *totally* rejected but it needn't. In fact, a rejection in one compartment of your life can add to your attraction in another.

The fact that your spouse walked out on you can result in your being freer and more flexible. This could perhaps make you a more desirable employee or job seeker.

You will be better able to manage your rejection if you don't talk about it to the wrong people. Remember, even though you've had a rejection in one area of your life, your integrity is still intact. But if you reject yourself, you can't expect others to accept you.

4. Study the Negative Qualities of the Person and/or Organization that Rejects You.

Their rejection could be the ultimate compliment. Maybe your creativity is wasted with them; perhaps they don't have the imagination to appreciate yours.

You will want to be extremely honest and fair in examining the mismatch. Don't be too ready to find the fault in the rejector instead of in yourself. Certainly bad-mouthing the one who rejects you is no solution.

But you can tell yourself—and come to believe it—that if "they" are dumb enough to reject you, "they'll" be sorry. Many rejectors are sorry, darned sorry.

Don't you suppose the Remington Arms Company regretted the decision to reject the rights to a patent owned by the Wagner Typewriting Machine Comany because "No mere machine can replace a reliable clerk"? As you already know by now, the Underwood Company was interested and proceeded to sell more than twelve million typewriters.

Anne Lindbergh gives an enchanting account of this approach to rejection in *Bring Me a Unicorn*. She made a serious attempt to study all of the negatives of the man with "that odious name, Lindy" because she wanted to prepare herself for possible rejection. In writing to her sister, Con, she said, "Lord, that man is cold, always on guard, with a one-track mind, and his coat doesn't fit." To herself, Anne said, "This is the solution: Don't say meekly and despondently, 'I have nothing in common with Colonel Lindbergh,' but flippantly and arrogantly say, 'Colonel Lindbergh has nothing in common with me.' "

Not only will you find negative qualities about some of those who reject you, you will also find there are those who look for negatives about anyone or anything. I swear there are those who could show you the down-side of heaven. Don't let them.

5. Learn From Rejection.

Rejection can help you to discover your weaknesses. This gives you the chance to convert those weaknesses to strengths.

How?

By enlisting the help of the person who rejects you.

If you're passed over for promotion, you must learn why. But you can't just ask "why?" or "what's wrong?" You can't because those questions are difficult for a manager to tackle. It's rough being a manager and one of the toughest aspects is looking a subordinate in the eye and leveling with that person.

You'll be far more effective if you'll express your genuine interest in strengthening your position and then ask for direction. No need for you to call attention to your weaknesses, but you will listen with attention (and without resentment) to suggestions for improvement.

You will, of course, be guarded about suggesting an "appraisal" interview. Your boss could welcome this opportunity to turn an appraisal interview into a termination interview.

You, of course, are trying to salvage what you can. You won't want to give up everything because you can't have it all.

If you're turned down for a job, you don't ask why either. You cut your losses; don't waste time or effort in a futile pursuit of that one job. But do ask the interviewer for some solid suggestions for strengthening subsequent interviews. While you're at it, it's also smart to ask for referrals. Personnel people know who's hiring.

"Why?" *is* a good question, and in the case of rejection—any rejection—ask *yourself* "why?" and try to come up with honest answers. If, after honest self-questioning, the rejection is still a mystery, ask a friend for *possible* suggestions.

As in the other situations, listen without resentment, and then put into action your program for improvement.

"YOU'RE FIRED"

Not working is the hardest job for almost everyone. But even the seemingly ultimate failure of job loss can be turned into a triumph if you handle it well.

While *you* might not be considering a job change, someone close to you might be involved with one; or, it's possible that somebody is considering a job change for you. Your boss, for instance.

Please continue with this chapter until you've absorbed all of it; let it be your insurance against future disappointment.

"You're fired." You don't need me to tell you how numbing, how devastating being fired can be. For many it's as painful as losing a loved one.

But it may be your chance to change your life. It can be—indeed, it often proves to be—an unexpected opportunity.

Bert Parks, who was fired as emcee for the Miss America pageant, says he is "looking for something else to be fired from" because so many opportunities have opened up for him since then.

The list of famous firees is long and includes Thomas A. Edison. Not only was Edison fired from the Grand Trunk Railway for accidentally setting the baggage car on fire with one of his chemical experiments, but the conductor also boxed his ears and threw him off the train, along with his chemicals and printing press.

Because you have nothing more to lose when a firing takes place, think about what you might have to gain. Your bargaining power is strongest at the moment of firing: this is the critical moment and the time for persuasion. Those responsible for wielding the ax feel the responsibility most keenly and are easiest to persuade at this time *if* you will act quickly.

First, find any written policies and implied promises in employee handbooks, and use them to help your employer "do what is right." Possible gains could include:

- more severance pay
- extension of benefits
- postponement of the actual termination date
- a letter of recommendation (yes, this is often forthcoming if requested—remind your employer of *what you have done well* and of *the times when you were a potent person*; such reminders serve *you* well at this time also)
- use of an office and clerical help during your search for a new position
- outplacement help

"You will be the guest of honor at a large company out placement party."

OUTPLACEMENT AND THE DISCREET DISMISSAL

Many companies cringe at the word *fired*. Dismissals must be discreet and they must seem voluntary on the part of the employee.

If you are anywhere near retirement age, you could be baited with early retirement; this leave-taking is often accompanied by an attractive pension or what is called the "golden parachute" or "golden handshake."

If you're not at retirement age or even approaching it, the more enlightened companies will offer professional job-search assistance or what we in the trade call *outplacement*.

What is outplacement?

Outplacement is providing placement help to a departing employee (one on the way *out*). Such help is usually limited to the employee who's getting what we might call an "honorable discharge." This help used to be reserved for top executives but what with all the mergers/acquisitions/company buy-outs, the practice now includes lower-echelon terminees as well.

Outplacement can cover everything from psychological counseling to interviewing techniques to résumé preparation. It can also include clerical service during the job hunt as well as office space and the use of a telephone.

Do I recommend outplacement?

Yes, for everybody. Outplacement reduces the trauma and tears that "dehiring" brings to employer and employee alike. Because it is a growing industry, there are still shortcomings. Outplacement firms vary greatly in skill and integrity. But the substandard practitioners are being weeded out by the ethical ones. Estimates are that the business is growing at an annual rate of 20 percent.

Suppose your company doesn't know about outplacement?

Ask for it anyway. If you are the victim of a discreet dismissal and you're being pressed to leave, cite these *employer* advantages. Make your comments general. You might mention that when help is offered in securing a new position for a departing employee, these benefits accrue:

• Bitterness toward the company is lessened.
• Secrecy agreements will be safer with a person who feels kindly toward the company he's leaving.
• There is less chance that customers will be solicited.
• Morale among remaining employees is strengthened.
• The company can be more realistic about severance pay—it often pays for itself by reducing compensation costs at separation time.
• The company's reputation for "fair play" is kept intact.

QUITTING YOUR JOB—GRACEFULLY

If your work situation is truly intolerable and you're thinking the unthinkable of "kissing your job good-bye," do just that.

Kiss it. Gently. There's no need to kick it. It's not dignified to have a temper tantrum on the way out the door.

Do

1. Give your present employer adequate notice.
2. Honor the terms of your contract—if you have one—or negotiate a release.
3. Offer to train a successor.
4. Be prepared to leave immediately if asked.
5. Ask for a letter of recommendation before you leave.
6. Send personal notes of thanks to your boss and associates if they've been supportive.
7. Inform the person who originally referred you to the job about your decision to leave.

Don't

1. Slam the door on the way out—you may want to re-enter through that same door.
2. Leap without a landing pad. You need to know where you're going before you go.
3. Let a single incident trigger your resignation.
4. Discuss your resignation with co-workers and others in your industry unless they are directly involved in your job change.
5. Use the threat of quitting as a bargaining tool with your present employer.
6. Cut the cord until you've checked on your benefit package with both your old and new employer. You need to know effective dates and dates of termination of benefits on all insurance and health care policies.
7. Return to gloat about your new assignment.

Part III
SELF-MAGNIFICATION

6

BECOMING AN

"ANOINTED ONE"

VISIBILITY

You can't expect to be promoted if nobody knows you're there.

As an advocate of your own career, you'll have to take charge of your own visibility.

While visibility leads to networking and networking leads to visibility, each is a separate concept and deserves special treatment. We'll get to networking in the next chapter. Right now let's talk about what you can do to become an "anointed one" in your area of operation.

Visibility tops the list. Fear of visibility—or false modesty—will keep you in obscurity.

Obviously, you can't brag about yourself, but you can say, "I've been told" and then spill some wonderful comments about yourself. And, you can encourage someone else to pass compliments about you on to your boss or your boss's boss. "Coming from someone like you, it will mean more" often steers a compliment to the desired target.

Before you include the following tips on visibility in your action plan, ask yourself about your company's profile.

Does your company nurture a low profile? If so, you will need to use subtlety and finesse in developing the image that works best where you are. Choose the best of the following tips; not all of them fit a low-profile organization.

Here are some easy and specific ways for you to become visible:

- Ask for more responsibility.
- Ask for and carry out special assignments. When you've worked on a special assignment—or even been responsible for a part of your boss's report—suggest that you present your segment of the work at the same time the boss makes a presentation. You do this, of course, to "spare" your boss the "added burden" of the more routine aspects of the job.
- Write a self-initiated analysis of an organizational problem.
- Write articles that show your competence in your field of work. Such articles could appear in your alumni or professional magazines. Reprints can then be sent to your company's publication. You will, of course, be wary about revealing sensitive material.
- Speak before groups—both inside and outside your organization. Create two speeches that travel. They don't have to be in your field—just be sure they're well-researched so that you have more information on the subjects than your audiences. Pick two topics you are enthusiastic about and that are timely and appropriate for a variety of audiences. Let program chairpersons know that your services/speeches are available. (Note: Public libraries in large metropolitan areas often publish Program Planner's Guides. These guides are developed as a public service. There is usually no charge to the group that uses the booklet nor to the speakers who are listed. Ask to have your name included.) Once you have a speaking assignment, cooperate with the club's publicity director by sending a black-and-white glossy photograph and a biographical sketch. You can even offer to write the news release.

Don't know how?

Back to the library for a booklet that tells you. Or ask for the media guidelines from the newspaper or station involved.

• If you have a specialty or interest that is "salable," offer your services to the local newspaper columnists, TV/radio talk show producers, and local TV access producers. Even if you don't get in print or on the show, you might be referred to or quoted.

• Participate in the meetings and conferences of your professional societies.

• Volunteer to run for office or to take a committee assignment for one of your professional societies.

• A dandy way to meet the movers and shakers in your field is to line up speakers for organizational meetings. If you snag such an assignment, do it with aplomb. You can strengthen your encounter with the speaker by sending details about the meeting, by acting as host *at* the meeting, and by sending a thank-you letter *after* the meeting. Never mind that the president or someone else in the organization has the responsibility for the official thank-you. An additional thank-you from you will always be welcome.

• Write in a newsletter—yours or somebody else's.

• Write a well-conceived letter to the editor. Before you send such a letter, have someone you trust check it for content and style.

• Send sincere congratulations to those who've earned them.

• Take leadership in community affairs. (Politics is a very chancy choice.) You might get on the board of a non-profit organization. There are many boards that don't attract the power people in the city (CEOs, philanthropists) but that are grateful to have lawyers, advertisers, accountants, media specialists, and other doers.

• Become active in your alumni association.

• Attend industry events such as trade shows.

• Let your boss know—in writing—about your accomplishments and about ideas you have for improving operations. Here are some specifics that can be measured and then cited to your superiors. Perhaps you can:
  • Cut costs by simplifying the delivery system; by doing a job more quickly and by teaching others to do it more quickly.
  • Increase safety.
  • Develop a security system or a better identification process.
  • Learn how to get government support and contracts.
  • Cut out unnecessary tasks.
  • Reduce inventories and storage space.
  • Make use of by-products.
  • Improve your product or the way the product looks.
  • Cut down on thievery and breakage.
  • Improve systems of reporting and exchanging information.
  • Solve a parking headache.
  • Report learning acquired at professional conferences.
  • Meet and beat deadlines.
  • Solve a personnel problem.
  • Become familiar with any new systems your company adopts. With every new system come bugs in the system. What are they? What can you do about it? Can the new system work more economically?

Expect to have some of the above techniques and suggestions result in your being invited to discussions with high-level managers. Often at a moment's notice.

When this happens, know who you are and what you can do. ALWAYS, always have an up-to-the-minute résumé or biographical sketch on yourself. This will clarify your thinking and it will help your management to view you in the light of current information.

Finally, remember that no one is more visible than the person in the limelight. When you're there, look your best.

SERENDIPITY

*Let your hook be always cast; in the pool where you
least expect it, there will be a fish.*

—Ovid

Serendipity is on your side. Expect to find it there. Marcus
Bach, author of *World of Serendipity*, describes it as "One of
life's sly and wonderful tricks." Or, ponder this definition of
serendipity that was given by Benjamin N. Cardozo, a Justice
of the Supreme Court: "Like many of the finest things of life,
like happiness and tranquility and fame, the gain that is most
precious is not the thing sought, but one that comes of itself in
the search for something else."

The faculty of making fortunate and unexpected discoveries is in all of us. But it's usually dormant because we
haven't trained ourselves to expect the unexpected. And *when
the unexpected is upon us, we don't see it.*

When you study the lives of the successful, you'll see that
serendipity was a factor in their success.

Alexander Fleming, the discoverer of penicillin, was certainly not the first scientist to experience spoiled mold spores
on culture plates. But he was the first to look deeply at what
was happening. He saw opportunity; others no doubt saw a
contaminated specimen.

Nor did Louis Braille let opportunity slip away. And, as a
result, millions of blind people can read. One day, while
playing a game of dominoes, Braille held one of those small,
black oblong tiles in his hand and mused, "Why not make an
alphabet of dots so that the blind may read by touch?"

Although I've thought seriously about serendipity and its
kinship with success for only a few years, I now realize that
this thing called chance—along with my innate optimism—
has played a magical role in my life.

Before I'd even heard the word, serendipity played a part in my developing an unusual job arrangement with a large retail store.

Along with hundreds of others, I'd applied for a summer job in order to earn money for college.

No, I didn't get the job. I didn't even get to meet the personnel director. But I was close enough to see her and to hear her name.

I saw her again shortly after that for she bought a dress from me. Oh yes, I persisted in my job search and was hired by another retailer. Naturally, I remembered the personnel director's name and I used it.

Surprised, she asked, "How in the world do you know my name?" I told her the story and she said, "If you still want to work for us, you can start next week."

"How about the week after?" I asked. "I need to train a replacement before I leave."

Not only did I get the job I wanted (it was closer to campus and paid more) but I was encouraged to log work time *whenever* my school schedule permitted. Sheer luck? I'm not sure.

Was it luck in the case of the woman's magazine editor who was in the waiting room when the employee she ultimately replaced stalked out in a fit of anger? The editor's friends all said, "Weren't you lucky to be sitting there at that moment?" "I don't know," the editor replied. "Seems to me I was in some editorial office on Madison Avenue *every* day. It was bound to happen some time."

Or, take the time my secretary made use of the unexpected. Not only did she make me look exceptionally bright but she stunned me anew with her sterling qualities and promotability.

By chance a college placement officer found herself with an unexpected half-day gap in her schedule. She decided to take this opportunity to call on Procter & Gamble with the hope of arousing my interest in her graduates.

The visit interrupted a dictation period. Instead of taking an emery board to her nails or using the "free" time in some way for herself, my treasure of a secretary realized that I wouldn't have a file on this particular college and would welcome background information. Moments before the placement officer and I headed for lunch, the secretary handed me an envelope marked "personal" and "urgent." In it were concise notes about the college, each bearing important information: enrollment figures, figures about how heavily the school was endowed and by whom, the name of its president, areas of specialization, founding date, and the names of well-known graduates.

Need I tell you what an impression I made on that placement officer? And need I tell you what an impression my secretary made on me? Small wonder the next appraisal on her almost went off the top of the appraisal sheet.

I have dozens of serendipity stories but my favorite is about the day I first met my husband.

My mission on that unforgettable day was to learn more about what went on in one of our technical buildings (some five miles from my office). Dutifully, I used the occasion to stop by the office of Dr. J. B. Martin in order to thank him personally for his referral of a candidate I'd hired. The outcome of that simple exercise in courtesy astounds me even now.

How does that serendipity definition go again? Something about "the faculty of making happy and unexpected discoveries by accident."

Marcus Bach believes that any one of us can be what he calls a "fate maker." And he's developed Bach's Law, which runs counter to that of Murphy's.

Bach's Law says: "If anything can go right, it must."

Try it; you'll like it.

HAVE YOU HUGGED YOUR BOSS TODAY?

The kind of hug I'm talking about is the psychological hug. NOT the physical one.

Often bosses are in need of positive support—psychological hugging—because they are in the line of fire. Top management expects them to carry out policy even when they're not always in agreement with it or permitted to explain it. Those below them often nurse their own "fear of the boss" instead of developing the fondness that could strengthen the relationship for both. And then there is the boss who *is* top management, the boss who's out there all alone, with no reinforcement from anybody.

Bosses are human beings; they also experience fear and feelings of inferiority.

If you have a boss, try to love her or him. Understand and respect the responsibilities he or she faces. An air of coolness and hostility sabotages any work, while care and concern produce harmony.

If you're male and your boss is a woman, take particular care to examine yourself for feelings of resistance or a desire to sabotage the effort. Her effort.

If your boss is considerably older or younger, it's up to you to give your boss the assurance that he or she is okay with you despite the age gap.

Regardless of the age or sex of your boss and no matter what your age or sex, there are guidelines to follow.

Here are the ten most important factors in the care and treatment of a boss:

1. *Ask for a chance to participate in setting your goals.* Then enlist your boss's support in carrying out your goals and those of your department. If you do so, you shouldn't find yourself in the position of having to go over the boss's head. Going over the boss's head should be considered in extreme situations only (with all the risk factors taken into account).

2. *Find out what your boss considers important.* When you know what your boss values, you'll be able to assign priorities to your assignments. After you've assigned priorities, do your tasks in the order of their importance.

3. *Give your boss progress reports at stated intervals* (mutually agreed upon). The more independent you want to be, the more information you must feed to the boss.

Be sure to include—in writing—personal accomplishments. Also include, with full credit to them, the accomplishments of your subordinates.

Bragging is out. Just report the facts: skills and techniques acquired, courses taken, recognition achieved. It is all right to pass along compliments paid to you or to your team.

4. *Give your boss the best performance of which you are capable.* While your boss is your boss, you must support him or her by doing the best job possible. To do anything less is unfair to both of you.

5. *Find out what your boss's major problems and responsibilities are.* Show your concern about them. Can you name five right now?

6. *Tell your boss when you like something.* Don't be the crank who speaks only when displeased.

7. *Do not surprise your boss.* Bosses don't like to be caught off guard. Even a pleasant surprise can have a negative impact if you "spring it" on the boss.

Don't have too many ideas and present them at odd times. Develop consistently good ideas and think them through before presenting them. Put them in writing and date them.

8. *Be the first to tell your boss about a major goof.* Then, almost in the same breath, ask for help. Say something such as, "I've blown it. Here's what happened. And here's what I'm doing as a stop-gap measure. But I need *your* help. What next?"

Don't vex your boss with trivia reports. Report your mistakes orally. You're a dodo if you document your mistakes in writing; such documentation could wind up in your personnel file.

9. *Be where your boss can find you.* How can you know how many times your boss looks for you if you're not around?

If you must leave, put an ETA on your desk and then return ahead of the time stated. You'll also want to be sure your phone is covered by a responsible person.

10. *Study your boss's management style.* Temper your response to that style by what you learn. Marlene Sanders, CBS correspondent, in an address before Women in Communications, Inc., noted that the management style of a male boss is often influenced by the women in his household, particularly his wife. A boss with a traditional wife tends to be protective, while a boss whose wife is career-oriented tends to value independence in a subordinate.

Hers is an important observation.

Your boss's style will be influenced by a number of factors: what kind of degree he or she holds (or doesn't hold), military background, quality of on-the-job experiences, and the management style of the boss's boss.

Now then, if, after following those ten guidelines, you still can't learn to love your boss, you must work to get that boss promoted. Within the organization preferably, but, if necessary, outside will do.

This requires real finesse, but if you're smart, you already know something about your boss's strengths. Reread the Visibility section—this time with your boss in mind. Train the spotlight on your boss's strengths.

If, despite your help, your boss's promotion doesn't seem imminent, put your dislike aside for a bit and take a downward look. At those below you in the pecking order.

Those under you can and should have a positive impact on your career. Do all you can to encourage their moves up the ladder. As they move, you move. For there you are, just a rung above. Dandy.

Now it's time to pay attention to how you perform in the role of boss.

Here are the ten most important factors in being a boss:

1. *Have your subordinates participate in setting appropriate goals.* Because they are closer to the task, ask for their observations and suggestions about accomplishing it. After targets have been agreed upon, define their responsibility and set a time frame for completion.

2. *Discover and make use of the strengths of those under you.* You can accomplish more by building on strengths than by trying to fit a worker into a preconceived mold.

3. *Give progress reports at stated intervals.* Tell your subordinates why a job needs to be done. Otherwise, the employee—like a computer—can only follow instructions instead of accomplishing the purpose.

Be candid about feedback; withholding information is not fair.

4. *Require good performance.* Our company physician once said, "Even if a man's unfaithful wife is driving him crazy, the boss should still insist upon the man's good performance at work. That way you keep him sane for at least eight hours a day."

Note: As long as a disability has no *necessary* impact on job performance, neither the disabled person nor the supervisor should permit it to have an impact on job performance.

5. *Reinforce good performance by rewarding it.* Give the reward sooner than expected. Under most merit systems the reward is too far removed in time from the event that triggered it to show an obvious relationship between performance and pay.

Note: Don't use "hard times" as an excuse to withhold a

reward. Be creative: Offer a day or half-day off, attendance at a professional meeting, or a chance to make a presentation to top management. Even a thank-you in writing makes a difference.

6. *Take responsibility for the mistakes of those under you while giving credit for their accomplishments.* You can't escape the responsibility of their mistakes and to try to do so makes you look weaker.

Calling attention to subordinates' strengths makes you look stronger to them as well as to your superiors.

7. *Delegate and do it deftly.* It's not fair to save all the stimulating assignments for yourself. Try for a neat balance between assigning tasks that don't merit your time and those that use your subordinates' strengths and add zing to work life.

8. *Never be overbearing with your subordinates.* They deserve your courtesy whether you're alone with them or in the presence of others. Observers should be able to figure out who's boss by the respect your subordinates accord you.

If you have a need to behave in an overbearing way, question your motivation. Insecurity? Revenge on a former boss?

9. *Negative criticism must be deserved and must be privately delivered.* With any negative criticism should come suggestions for improvement.

Arthur Godfrey, probably the most popular entertainer on early television, gave a dramatic lesson on how not to be a boss. On October 19, 1953, he fired a member of his "family" of regulars, young Julius LaRosa. Just as "Julie" finished singing "I'll Take Manhattan," Godfrey told him he had just sung his "swan song."

That firing caused such a furor that Mr. Godfrey's "congeniality" image was forever tarnished. To say nothing of his ratings.

10. *Do team building where it is appropriate.* You'll want to be in tune with management's strategy on this one.

ROCK OF SAGES

Why should I be totally original? I read a lot, I listen a lot, and I absorb a lot.

When the material is good, I have a strong urge to pass it on. That's how this segment was born.

What you see here are the rock-hard basics—the unchangeable rules in a changeable world. These are the pungent remarks and solid ideas of "sages" concerning achievement, hence the title "Rock of Sages." Honesty forces me to admit that I slipped in a few of my own gems. Why not? I've hoarded, polished, suffered over, and savored some of these messages for years.

I'll start with my all-time favorite. It's borrowed from Albert Schweitzer:

> *I do not know what your destiny will be, but one thing I know; the only ones among you who will be truly happy are those who will have sought and found how to serve.*

Next, let's hear from the person I consider the best-informed American of our time, Ann Landers:

> *Anyone who says the days of opportunity are over is copping out.*

And:

> *Nobody ever drowned in his own sweat.*

Judith Bogart, the second woman ever to be the national president of the Public Relations Society of America, cites advice her mother gave her:

> *Always do more than is expected of you and you will be a success. . . .*

The reward from work is not what you get from it, but what you become by it.

Barbara Proctor, advertising tycoon:

Take risks. You can't fall off the bottom.

And:

If you make only right turns you'll be going in circles.

How will you know when you've reached the power level, the level of authority? Others in authority will recognize it in you. There is an unmistakable signal; it will pass between you.

Barbara A. Pletcher, Executive Director of the National Association for Professional Saleswomen:

The real winners in life are the people who look at a situation with an expectation that they can make it work or make it better.

Jeffrey G. Allen, author of *How to Turn an Interview into a Job*, on success:

Imperceptible nuances make the difference—the right time and other variables.

Ideas are precious. Whenever you spawn an idea, take good care of it. Write it down and if you show it to another, be sure your name is on it and that it's dated. Also, be sure that the person who sees the paper knows that you've shown it to others of power.

Thomas Carlyle, the historian and philosopher, wrote this in 1843:

> *Blessed is he who has found his work. Let him ask no other blessedness.*

Philip Guedalla:

> *Success is little more than a chemical compound of man with moment.*

Jane Evans (in addressing a conference of attendees at the annual meeting of the International Association for Personnel Woman):

> *Until we women can in large numbers say, "My career is what I am and it comes first," we are not going to crash the barriers which are keeping us out of the executive suite and on the second string of the management team.*

Mary Cunningham:

> *Winners have the ability to adapt to the terrain.*
> *They blend practicality with idealism.*
> *They take responsibility for their own career path.*

The comment that follows is an excellent one to share with the boss who has failed to note—and reward—your increased value to the organization. George Bernard Shaw:

> *The only person who behaves sensibly is my tailor. He measures me anew each time he sees me.*

Hannah Moore:

> *Obstacles are those frightful things you see when you take your eyes off the goal.*

Arthur Schopenhauer:

To overcome difficulties is to experience the full delight of existence.

Victoria Sackville-West:

There is scope for inventiveness everywhere if only we have the vision to perceive it. The breakers-away are the creators.

Karen Hendricks, Associate Director, Procter & Gamble:

Successful people are so labeled because they have a string of accomplishments to their names. Interestingly, they also have a string of failures. The successful person has converted these setbacks to positive experiences that become springboards to their success.

James A. Garfield:

If the power to do hard work is not talent, it is the best possible substitute for it.

Elbert Hubbard:

It is a fine thing to have ability, but the ability to discover ability in others is the true test.

Frances Parkinson Keyes:

Hunt for the difference that makes a difference.

James Thurber:

It is better to ask some of the questions than to know all the answers.

Myron Cohen:

> *If you work hard and keep both feet on the ground, you'll eventually reach a point at which you'll be able to put both feet on a desk.*

Bernie Weiner, Vice President, U.S. Shoe Corporation:

> *No failure in life is as final as the failure to find out what you do best.*

Even success is bitter when it is slow in coming.

Branch Rickey:

> *Luck is the residue of design.*

And I can't resist this one; *New York Mirror* scribe Frances Merron is responsible:

> *No man goes before his time. Unless, of course, the boss leaves early.*

7

THE N'TH DEGREE

NEGOTIATING: IT PAY$

I know better than to talk about the kind of negotiating that involves labor contracts. Negotiating with a union or negotiating a formal contract requires a specialist or agent.

That lets me out.

But I do know that almost everybody is involved in negotiating *on* the job as well as *for* the job. And I do know ways to make this negotiating more fruitful and to make you look more professional.

Because most people don't know what they want out of life—let alone out of a career—the negotiating technique is rarely developed.

How you ask for what you want can set you apart from others and can call attention to how special and professional you are. Remind yourself that you won't become an "anointed one" by needless apology and tentative language. Your anointment will come about when you follow careful negotiating techniques such as those set forth for you here.

Let's start with the basis of all negotiation: *Know what you want before you ask for it.*

In many instances, what you want is not money. Worker surveys corroborate my experience concerning this premise. Oh sure, money is important and we'll talk about it because money is the way you keep score. Certainly it's the way management keeps score. In fact, I hear some members of management saying, "If you can't count it, it doesn't count."

But bear with me for a few minutes and we'll get to negotiating for dollars as well as bartering for things that mean more to you than a fistful of money.

For the purpose of zeroing in on what you really want, Dr. Min Basadur of Hamilton University, Ontario, has developed a simple but powerful method.

If you'd like to try it, here's my modified version. Ask yourself what you want to do, see, own, or have. No matter how trivial your desire might be, jot it down.

Participants in my workshops have mentioned these:

- a job
- a promotion
- to spend time in Hawaii
- to have power
- to have an extended vacation
- to have a private office
- to be on television
- to have a book published
- to become a national sales director for Mary Kay
- to own a Corvette
- to learn to fly
- to have a baby
- to get married
- to become a life master at bridge
- to climb the Matterhorn
- to get a degree
- to win the lottery
- to play a respectable round of golf

After the participants have jotted down (quickly) about fifteen items, I ask them to attach values to what is there. If the list contains fifteen desires, I ask them to put an *A* after the five most compelling desires, a *B* after the next five most compelling desires, and to label those that remain as *C* items.

Then I ask that they draw a line through all *C* items and forget about them. Why go after something that is not a high priority? By narrowing and defining your target, you're setting goals.

What are goals anyway?

They're just dreams written down.

Next comes the important part: how to seek help in achieving your goals. Negotiating. Barter.

What follows is not a summation of all I've read or heard on the subject; it's not even a summation of all I've written or presented in speeches. But the guidelines here are key ones. Study them carefully and you won't go into a negotiating session unarmed and you certainly won't come out empty-handed.

Thirteen Keys to Successful Negotiating

1. Clarify your goals. Be able to express, at least to yourself, "This is what is important to me." Think about specific considerations (in addition to money) that are important. Considerations such as:

- shorter or more flexible hours
- better physical surroundings
- a private office (in order to do better work; to conduct sensitive interviews)
- time to pursue special training
- tuition coverage
- company-paid attendance at industry meetings
- company-paid membership in a professional organization
- attendance at in-house training sessions
- a better vacation package
- health/dental/life insurance

- an expense account
- club membership
- one's own parking space

2. Be sure to negotiate with the right person.

3. Be sure you're underpaid. When the budget gets tight, the most expensive deadwood is cut first. Instead of blithely asking for *more* money, ask yourself, "Are they getting their money's worth out of me? Do they know they're getting their money's worth out of me?" Finally, "Am I worth more?"

Please hear me out on this: I am not saying settle for a low salary. You can earn a salary well into six figures and be underpaid in relation to your contribution. Just make sure you're worth whatever you seek.

4. Never ask for a raise because you need one; need should not be mentioned. You negotiate for more money only after you've earned it. Even then, plain old *asking* is out.

5. It's better to ask for more responsibility than it is to ask for more money.

6. Never negotiate on the past. Stress the value you represent now and will continue to represent.

7. Know what you are worth in the marketplace. Find out the "going rate" for what you do:

- from colleagues in the same field
- from figures compiled by the Labor Department of the federal government and by your state Bureau of Employment Services
- from salary surveys made by your professional society (Such studies are published in professional journals. Your librarian can pin these down for you. While you're at the library, ask for current salary survey information from newspapers and other periodicals.)

Know what your management could pay and still get a good deal. When you name a figure, be prepared to tell how you arrived at it. You'll be more successful if you know when the new budget period begins and make your move early in the new period.

8. Have your appraisal on yourself ready:
- date and amount of last increase
- training undertaken and completed
- money earned or saved for the company
- plans for additional savings when you're promoted
- extra assignments completed
- outline of your suggestions that were adopted

9. Think of negotiating as a "win-win" situation. You win and management wins. Be prepared to tell management what their gains will be. Have a specific gain to fit each request. For example:
- If you ask for flextime, talk about how much more you accomplish by working at your peak-efficiency times.
- If you ask for more responsibility, emphasize the reduced stress on the boss. (Note: First you must know what the boss's responsibilities are.)
- If you talk money, give specific examples of how you will be worth more than the amount invested in you.

10. Don't be afraid of silence. And don't be afraid to say, "I don't know enough about the job [or the promotion] at this stage. May we talk money a bit later when I know more?"

11. Don't be afraid to be the first to name a figure. It's important to get "them" thinking of you in terms of the highest—but reasonable—figure. Name a range, rather than a tight figure, but start with the highest range you might be able to command. *Down you can always come.*

You might say: "Judging from what you tell me about the importance of this job, I'd guess the range to be about _____?" If the figure causes the other person to fall over the back side of the chair, you'll know you were a bit high. At which point, you say, "I'm sure you had a range in mind?"

Know that an employer's first figure is not necessarily the final offer.

12. Prepare your boss for an appraisal and be prepared for more than one session.

Plan the setting. You do not corner the boss at the water cooler nor do you invite the boss to dinner for the purpose of asking for a raise. Crass. In fact, *you do not invite the boss to dinner at all* unless your boss has indicated yours is to be a social relationship as well as a business one. Even then, the boss issues the first invitation.

13. Don't go away empty-handed. Have more money or a concession. As a minimum, have the promise of a salary review in a shorter period of time than usual.

If your negotiation is with a future employer, try to get something in writing. If the employer is nervous about providing a letter of intent, you might write a note outlining the conditions of the position you think you are accepting. Then ask, "Are we in agreement on this?"

Is all this risky?

You bet. But the prizes go to the risk takers. You'll never win a contest you were afraid to enter.

NETWORKING: THE POWER OF POSITIVE LINKING

I believe strongly in the "network" concept but fear the word *networking* is working too hard. And so are some of the dear souls who agree to become a part of someone's network.

One weary executive, an ex-networker, cornered me after my talk at the Nashville Career Conference to say, "Put me down for a copy of your new book. I want one provided you include this message: Networking is out, out, out." He caught up with me still later to add, "My friends are getting fed up with it, too, so lay it on the line with your readers." It seems the poor man had managed to get on a list for informational interviews and some interviewees had abused his courtesy.

Despite his comments and the probable loss of a book sale, I still say: Use—but do not abuse—networking, linking, bonding, or whatever you choose to call it. It works when it's correctly used.

I wrote this segment to remind you of the ways achievers now use networking and to stimulate you to use your creativity to forge ahead by linking to powerful people and concepts. Your chances for anointment are greatly strengthened when your network is broad enough to include decision makers from *both* inside and outside your organization. Indeed, many of the anointed were brought to the attention of their own management by a decision maker from outside. And, of course, any link that provides you with more information and better information enables you to do a better job. It follows that better performance makes you a candidate for promotion.

After reading and adapting the guidelines set forth here, you will be using not only the established links but links *no one else* uses. Links that others haven't even considered.

Nine Keys to Positive Linking

1. This is a basic lesson: Employers hire in their own image and managers promote those who are most like them. Ask yourself: Which person up there could look at herself or himself and see *me*? Then be sure to include that person in your linking.

How?

You might invite such a senior executive to join you at a meeting. Be in tune for, have your antennae out to receive, messages about where it makes sense to issue such an invitation; indeed, where failure to do so could seem an oversight. If, for example, you learn your professional organization plans to feature a speaker from the senior executive's alma mater, it would be thoughtful to extend an invitation to the executive.

Don't invent a reason and don't use as a reason the fact that you're looking for an "in" with the power person.

There must be genuine concern and respect for the person with whom you link. The test to determine this requires you to ask: Would I welcome the chance to do a favor for this person even if circumstances prevented him or her from learning I'm responsible? *and*: Would I break the bonds linking me to this person if he or she fell from power?

2. To be truly effective, linking—or whatever term you use—must be creative. Think of all the strings that bind you to others and consider ways to strengthen the ties. Creative ways.

I have an effective exercise I use with my job hunters; I call it *"Know* Strings Attached." (They call me "Attila, the Hun" because of my persistence in executing it.)

The exercise needn't be limited to the job search. I'm telling you about it because you can apply the principle and make it work in almost any situation. Here's how I do it: I use an instant camera to take a picture of each seminar attendee. I slap each little photo onto the center of a large, blank sheet of paper. Then I attach strings to the picture (actually from it) and have the job seekers assign names to the strings.

The names?

Anyone the job seekers might know or know about who could steer them to job leads. I have them—force them— to include the names of their attorney, doctor, banker, minister, grocer, druggist, mail carrier, elected officials (especially those at the local level), fellow alumni, former teachers and professors, fellow service veterans, friends of spouse, parents, and other relatives. And wait till you hear this: *everybody* whose name could be used to form a bond.

For example, I say to the person whose name is Adams: "Have you been in touch with every person of power in this town whose name is Adams? Okay, off to the City Directory (*not* the phone directory) with you. Let's see what all those Adamses do. Then make appointments with all those who could help."

You'd be amazed at how easy it is for an Adams to get through to another Adams. So help me, I'm quoting a man named Adams who called me to say, "It works! I followed up on seventeen prospects and have eight appointments. Never mind that they're all named Adams."

I've now broadened this exercise to have Bears get in touch with Foxes, Cranes with Peacocks, Browns with Greens, and so on.

For those whose last name is a first name—such as Howard—the thing to do is get in touch with the Arnolds, the Pauls, the Dicks, etc. A person whose surname is Arnold does not misfile a James or Howard or forget the name—particularly if a point is made of it.

You have a long, unpronounceable name? Simple. Find someone else who also has.

Does this work?

Dear ones, when my job seekers follow those strings, they *have* jobs before the sessions on *how to find them* are over.

3. The linking should go up and down and move laterally. And, like exercise, it's easier to do if it's done regularly. Only then do the links form a strong, secure bond—the foundation of a solid and lasting network.

4. Consider joining a formal network, both locally and at the national level. Yes, there are networks of networks. So many I couldn't begin to name them here (and more are cropping up as I write this). Your Chamber of Commerce can tell you what's available in your area. And your local network groups can link you to the national ones.

5. Be selective in the use of your network. Don't aimlessly collect business cards or bombard a city with résumés. Put some thought behind it; name dropping works but only if it fits.

6. Include in your linking those who *can't* help you. In particular, make it a habit to praise service that is exceptionally good—in writing if at all possible. Written comments become part of the person's personnel record. This is the way we keep caring people on the job; when we do that, everybody benefits.

7. The linking must be a confirmation of your contributions to that which you believe in.

8. Seek sponsorship. Every wise person seeks a link with those who are wiser still.

These wise ones—be they mentors, angels, godmothers, or godfathers—can, as Karen Hendricks of Procter & Gamble puts it, "catapult us into positions we could not otherwise reach. But we have to learn to ask for advice and support."

Also from Karen: "Mentors, like wished-for fathers and mothers, guide us in how we present, position, and connect ourselves." They are the source of special clues or privileged information that only veterans know; they can alleviate some of the pain in learning the "politics" of the workplace.

You will be wise to seek help for the task, not personal help. You'll also be wise to have more than one mentor. Some experts say, "Get yourself a board of directors." Not too bad an idea. I'm still haunted by a remark I heard fifteen years ago. This is it, verbatim: "He was Harry's boy, but Harry's gone. Haw, haw." The guffaw is still audible, too.

Certainly your having more than one mentor makes it easier on the mentor. Not that *you* would rely on someone for *advice on everything*.

9. Consider after-hours activities as a means to effective linking.

In order to demonstrate how effective such linking can be, I'm now making use of a bond I developed with another Martin. Bruce, my husband, insists you wouldn't be interested in a speech he made on "After-Hours Activities: Shortening the Corporate Ladder."

I insist you would.

If you are, please continue with an adjunct to this chapter. This speech was delivered at a conference of the American Institute of Chemical Engineers in Chicago, Illinois, and appeared in *Chemical Engineering Progress* in July 1981. I have Bruce's permission and that of Larry Resen, editor and publisher, to show it to you.

AFTER-HOURS ACTIVITIES: SHORTENING THE CORPORATE LADDER

Can you help your career by being elected to the school board, becoming chairman of your local section, heading a hospital fund drive, or running a marathon in 2:43? That depends on whether there is congruity between the after-hours activity and your career. Each of these activities can be worth your while on its own merit, but the effect on your career could be positive, negative, sideways, or neutral. It all depends on how well the activity fits your personal career path. If it fits, it moves you along. If it doesn't fit, it has no effect, slows you down, or pushes you off.

I plan to discuss this subject in terms of five congruities:

• Congruity with personal goals
• Congruity with the company
• Congruity with the job
• Congruity of image
• Congruity with priorities

I'll explain each of these terms as I discuss it. The sequence is just for convenience in developing ideas and is not intended to suggest the order of importance. Personally, however, I think that the first, congruity with personal goals, *is* the most important.

If you don't care where you are going, any path will get you there. Of course, you may then not like where you are. If your goal is to climb a managerial ladder, the appropriate after-hours activities to advance toward that goal will be somewhat different from those appropriate to climbing the technical ladder. Continuing education is an obvious example. Because of tuition refund plans or other support of employee education, continuing education is not an anonymous activity. Some universities even report honors lists, etc., to employers. Your choice of continuing education courses is certainly a signal to your superiors, and your performance in them may attract attention. Obtaining an MBA conveys a very different message from taking a series of highly technical courses.

Perhaps your goal does not involve climbing the corporate ladder at all. Mobility may be more important to you. In that situation, the important visibility for you may lie outside the company. You may find that trade or professional organizations offer the platform you need.

Intention to remain mobile is not the only reason for placing emphasis on other goals than climbing ladders. There appears to be a trend today toward recognizing, accepting, and rewarding people who perform other roles in the organization. Status defined as position on a ladder is far less important to some people than is autonomy. After-hours activities that foster autonomy are those which are valued by the company—about which I will say more in a moment—but which are not appropriate for control by the company. Political activity and professional society activity are likely to fit here.

The second congruity I mentioned is congruity with the company. By this I mean being involved in an activity which the company supports. A good indication of which activities are likely to fit is to see what organizations the executives of the company work with. If a company executive heads this year's United Fund drive, and you turn in an outstanding performance for a unit of the drive, you necessarily get some notice. But there is a trap here—excellence may be the norm, and you may put in an inordinate amount of effort just to not look bad.

Since this is a meeting of AIChE, I would like to comment specifically on technical society activity. The fit for a technology company—and I include much of the chemical industry in that category—is very good. Company executives are likely to be personally involved and to be interested in the activities of their subordinates. In a company serving broader markets, the effect may be somewhat different. I can offer a personal example on this point. I have been very active in technical societies while working for a company which is best known for its consumer products. My activities have been recognized, appreciated, and supported. But my reward has been freedom to pursue these interests, not rungs up a ladder.

It might be easy to misread the membership of company executives on boards of hospitals, foundations, or civic organizations. Those memberships may be the effects, not causes, of progress in the company. I have seen several that seemed to "go with the territory."

There are risks in being highly visible in support of controversial causes. You could be an embarrassment to your company. And, should you publicly advocate a position that is a threat to your company's business, your own corporate ladder may suddenly become very short.

The term, "congruity with the job," as I am using it, really means the fit between the capabilities demonstrated in the after-hours activities and the capabilities required for the job to which you wish to advance. Some examples are obvious. If you are striving for a management position, the successful management of a complex operation—such as a civic celebration—shows abilities needed for the position you want. Or if you really want a faculty position, an adjunct professorship is a step in that direction.

Perhaps there are some general qualities which are good for almost any position, and it can't hurt to bring these to the attention of those who have influence on our career; but I think it is unrealistic to think that great things will happen because you have won a tennis tournament or a Toastmaster's award.

Golf must be in a class by itself. The only explanation I can offer for the obvious relevance of golf is that the minuscule portion of the elapsed time spent in hitting the ball leaves a tremendous amount of time for conversation. The golf course, therefore, becomes a place for delicate negotiations. Some skill at golf seems directly applicable to jobs requiring cultivation of contacts. On the basis of anecdotal data, I suspect that one should be good, but not too good, at the game.

Congruity of image means being involved in ways that support the image you want to present to people who have influence on your career. Do you want to be viewed as a professional? Publications, presentations of papers, and professional society activities support that image. On the other hand, these same activities may very well suggest a lack of interest in the managerial ladder.

Unfortunately, women still need to be particularly conscious of image. Sexism that is officially frowned upon at work has a way of cropping up in after-hours activities. A man heading a hospitality committee may be seen as an organizer, while a woman in the same position may be expected to bake cookies.

For both women and men, the nature of their after-hours activities can convey strong messages about their attitudes toward their careers. To paraphrase the old advice about how to take psychological tests, I suppose the "right" position is: "I love my vocation and my avocation, but my vocation a little more."

There are also a number of less clearly defined dimensions for the image from after-hours activities:

- Progressive or conservative
- Rebel or establishment
- Stable or mobile
- Leader or follower

Sometimes the question of image is even more subtle. Consider sports, for example. I know of one medium-sized company in which a person's position and status can be inferred quite accurately by noting whether a person is a golfer, a bowler, or a softball player.

Congruity of image, of course, is not clearly separated from congruity with personal goals, with the company, and with the job.

The fifth congruity I mentioned is congruity with priorities. This is simply the question of other options for the use of the same time. You can't do everything, so you have to choose.

In closing, I want to make two more points. This is not in summary, because I haven't said these before:

1. The most important influence on your career is performance on the job, not what you do off the job.
2. The effect on your career is not the most important factor in deciding how to spend your time off the job.

8

ANTICIPATION: WHAT IS

THIS WORLD COMING TO?

Would that I could interpret all the handwriting on the wall.
But there's so much there on the wall, the wall's about to fall.

If you won't fidget too much about a seeming lack of
direction, I'll get to the part that fits the purpose of the book:
your personal empowerment. Because knowledge is power,
you must incorporate in your general store of knowledge
information about what to expect in the future. It's this
forward look that earns you the reputation of being a "comer"
or, as we call it, an "anointed one."

I'll provide solid information about *some* of what you can
expect in the next five to ten years that could influence the
direction your career takes.

But the person who's in the best position to predict what's
going to happen is the person who's going to make it happen.
YOU. The words to the song, "Whatever will be, will be"
needn't be your refrain.

My observations are based on—what else?—observation.
Because I'm a reporter to my marrow, I've researched every
observation I mention here. I invite you, actually urge you, to
do the same. Let my investigative instincts arouse yours.

For instance, don't dismiss what I say about the *permanence* of temporary work because you don't choose to believe me. Instead, do as I so often do (and have done in more than twenty-five major cities): go to your phone directory and look at the number of employment contractors listed in the Yellow Pages. As you probably already know, employment contractors are the people who "contract" with employers to supply needed temporary help.

Compare the number of contractors you see today with the listing of ten years ago. Your telephone company has old directories and so do many libraries. After you get over the shock of how much the list has grown in the past ten years, ask yourself what that growth indicates for the future.

But please don't stop there; look in the classified advertising section of today's newspaper under the heading "Help Wanted, Temporary." Now compare it with your newspaper's classified ad section for ten years ago (in the newspaper's "morgue"). Even though you may see more job openings listed in the old newspaper, I'll give odds you find more "temporary" listings in today's paper.

Lest I get too wordy about some of the ways I back up my predictions, I'd better get on with the business of giving you a smattering of the actual predictions.

1. *There is nothing temporary about the trend toward temporary work.* I see—and expect to see more—people in all types of jobs and at all levels of jobs in temporary assignments. I'm talking about those with degrees and advanced degrees as well as lower-echelon workers.

I'll say, and I hope you quote me, that in about five years, a whopping one-fourth to one-third of us will be classified as consultants, freelancers, temporaries, or part-timers.

Why?

Here are some of the more compelling reasons:

- The rapid changes in technology make many workers obsolete. Employers must have access to those who are up on the latest technology. One way is to hire them as

consultants instead of putting them on the regular pay-
roll.

- It is cost-effective. Employers have been forced to cut
down on the back-breaking costs of the "benefit package"
accorded the permanent employee. The person on a temporary assignment is paid only for the time worked and
usually does not receive fringe benefits.
- Recent economic swings have alerted employers to the
danger of overstaffing.
- Mergers and aquisitions of companies are at an all-time
high and *will increase*. As a result of so many "M & A's"
the "new" company often revamps, retrenches, fires, and
sometimes rehires (as consultants) those who've been
released.
- Temporary hiring is one way to skirt the "discrimination
trap." Employers tell me (privately) that they are afraid
to ask all the questions they need to ask in order to make
good hiring decisions. Furthermore, when they do give
someone a permanent assignment and the person doesn't
work out, they have "the devil's own time" firing the
unsatisfactory employee. The obvious answer is to "try
before you buy." I am aware that as I write this, legisla-
tors are trying to halt this kind of "temporary" employment.

2. *A global view will become a necessity.* You already know
we're in a worldwide communication explosion and those of
us who don't or won't learn about computers, word processing, and telecommunications will have the same handicaps
the illiterate person now has.

But have you considered how foreign ownership has increased—and is continuing to increase? Does this affect your
business? Could it affect your business? If so, will you be able
to communicate with the foreign owners of your business?

3. *Spanish, along with English, will become an official U.S.
language.* Probably within the next five years. Have you no-

ticed the increased number of Spanish-speaking elected officials? And have you noticed the wooing of the "Hispanic vote" in the current elections? Have you noticed Spanish instructions in the phone directories of major cities? No, I'm not limiting the question to cities such as Miami, Los Angeles, and San Antonio, where you might expect to see both Spanish and English. I'm talking about mid-American cities such as Chicago. Incidentally, the voting instructions for Chicagoans already appear in Spanish as well as English.

And now that I've seen the Spanish version of Bugs Bunny, I am a believer in my own prediction.

What does this mean to your job success? It means that it would be very wise to ask yourself what new regulations this will bring about. For instance, will your business forms have to be in Spanish as well as English?

4. *Knowledge of sign language will be a plus to the upward bound.* I firmly believe that knowing how to sign will serve as an open door to many opportunities. I expect to see "with it" banks, television stations, restaurants, churches, and service organizations reaching out to the hearing impaired.

5. *There will be water wars.* I expect to see a water crisis that will rival the oil crisis of the '70s.

Why am I writing this in a book about job success? Because the reader with real moxie will reflect on this prediction and turn it to advantage. That person will realize an unhampered water supply is as important to his or her company's lifeblood as water is to the human body.

Such a person will go beyond the "ain't it awful" response and say, "Hey, maybe *I* could become a water consultant. Perhaps I could parlay my legal knowledge [or knowledge of real estate, geology, or engineering] into a specialty that would increase my value."

No doubt about it, the need for fresh water will affect not only the *kinds of jobs* that are created in the next few years buy also *where the jobs are.* Water should give some of the depressed areas of the country (near the Great Lakes) the bargaining chips to deal with the Sunbelt states that need those precious drops of water.

The federal courts have already been called upon to referee some squabbles over diverting the course of water.

6. *Expect to see gambling casinos in major cities.* You're already seeing more lotteries and legalized gambling. Soon, many cities will turn to casino gambling as a way out of their financial problems. Like it or not, such activity spawns jobs. Publicists for Atlantic City claim that each casino there creates three thousand jobs.

7. *Expect to see more employee buy-outs/takeovers.* While such buy-outs and takeovers are not widespread, they are expected to increase. Dr. William Whyte, professor emeritus of industrial relations at Cornell University and a student of employee takeovers, reports that more than 50,000 jobs have been saved in nearly sixty takeovers in the past ten years.

Certainly workers will become more involved in problem solving and in decision making. Such worker involvement is one of the ways of stemming the loss of the smokestack industries.

8. *Expect to see more industrial bartering.* Many companies now say that barter is smarter. Estimates are that as many as 67 percent of major companies are involved in barter of goods and/or services.

9. *Expect to see staggering advances in medicine.* The marriage of medicine and high technology is so advanced and so intertwined it's difficult to put separate headings on some of the predictions, but you will see:

- Computers used in birth control. The technology is already here.
- Parents deciding on the sex of their child (before conception).
- Tiny computers that will tell us how many calories we've burned since our last meal.

- It is likely there will be nuclear techniques that will make X rays obsolete.
- "Life Extenders" predict maximum lifespan increases; some say we will extend our lifespan to 125 years or more.

10. *The trend in the growth of small business is expected to continue.* Analysts estimate that the number of entrepreneurs has doubled in the last ten years. Small wonder then that so many job opportunities are developing in emerging industries. According to the Department of labor, 80 percent of the new jobs are now in small business.

11. *The rental concept is expected to expand.* Right now if you can name it you can probably rent it. It's possible to rent job-seeking outfits—and, are you ready?—party guests and demonstrators.

Wait. I'm still not finished: Employers are renting employees. Yes, employee leasing is gaining in popularity. Many owners of small- and medium-sized businesses find employee leasing a way out of labor problems and bookkeeping headaches. And leasing employees provides a tax advantage to the employer.

In a sense, the business owner hires an employee-leasing company to hire, manage, and fire its employees—for all practical purposes to act as a personnel (human resources) department. Though the practice is in its infancy, employee-leasing companies are growing at a staggering rate. Don't panic. Employee-leasing companies can offer benefits similar to those of the large companies.

12. *More government involvement is predicted for agencies and businesses.* The upward bound will need to know *how* government affects their operations. Specifically, regulations involving occupational safety, environmental safeguards, waste disposal, and equal opportunity. You should also know what grants and loans are available and how to get them for your organization.

13. *Experts say many "new" jobs will replace the old ones.*

The smart money is on those individuals who know this and catch a field in its infancy.

I expect to see opportunities for:

- those who develop "toys" for adults (designed for the talented upper-echelon part-timers who need to be entertained in their leisure hours)
- laser specialists—from the technician in industry up to and including the laser surgeon
- those in the robotics field
- management-information-systems specialists
- those in health care (including biomedical technology and areas such as geriatric social work)
- telecommunications
- business/marketing
- engineering
- materials utilization
- hazardous waste management
- those involved with energy (including nuclear and solar sources)
- battery technicians
- food service

All of the above represents a mere sampling of what's to come.

Relax. Knowing some of what's ahead will reduce stress; it's unfamiliarity with the possibilities that gets us.

To fight the future (or change) is to *lose*. To be passive is at best a *tie*. To accept the challenge of change—to actually help shape the future—is to *win*.

9

SUMMATION: THE SEVEN

CARDINAL VIRTUES

There are big virtues just as there are big sins. The seven highlighted here are virtues that matter for you take-charge types who want to control your own career paths.

I went to considerable trouble to confine the conversation in this chapter to *C* topics. I did it in order to make this, the review chapter, easy to remember and easy to internalize. Just think of the "seven *C*'s." The substance of the book's message is here for you in capsule form.

Up to this point we've concentrated largely on *what to do* to become an "anointed one"; now we talk about *what to be*. What to become.

If you want to be soaringly successful, be *challenging*, be *charming*, be *committed*, be a *communicator*, be *confident*, be *creative*, and be *current*.

While the acquisition of these seven *C*'s won't take the place of the two or three letters after your name, such acquisition will assure your solid success.

THE SEVEN C's

1. Be *challenging*. Take risks, but don't let risk become rash. There's no point in flirting with danger by ignoring rules and shunning advice. Know the price of your action and be willing to pay it.

High reward goes with high risk but it's downright foolish to function outside your area of competence. However, you limit yourself needlessly if you don't *extend* your area of competence.

David Lloyd George expressed all this rather well when he said, "Don't be afraid to take a big step if one is indicated. You can't cross a chasm in two small jumps."

2. Be *charming*. Your best personality is the one that's already inside you. Free that personality; then forget yourself enough to be yourself.

Forgetting yourself is the beginning of awareness of others. It is this awareness, this lack of "self-centeredness," that leads to "other-centeredness" and to charm.

The late Adlai Stevenson, himself a charmer, came up with the best description of charm I've heard. When asked if he noticed beautiful women, Mr. Stevenson replied, "I always notice a beautiful woman but I prefer a charming one. She notices *me*."

I would add to that observation some encouraging news about charm or "personal chemistry." *It can be learned.* So reports Handy Associates, the nation's oldest executive-search firm. This personal chemistry or charm is a combination of appeal to the senses (reread the "Come to Your Senses" chapter) and deliberate thoughtfulness. Thoughtfulness that schools you to remember the names and interests as well as the tender spots of those you meet.

Here are techniques in thoughtfulness that can enhance your charm:

- Develop a card file for acquaintances, business associates, and friends. Carry three-by-five cards with you to record names you want to remember. Add addresses, phone numbers, name of spouse, ages and names of children, hobbies and interests as the information becomes available.

People are "charmed" when you remember them and their

concerns. An added advantage: a card file is easier to keep current than an address book.

The "new kid" in the department can become an instant hit this way. No, don't show the file. It is for your eyes only.

- Tread tenderly on the sore spots of others. Learn that "saving face" is a saving grace.

Those brought up in oriental cultures know the importance of saving face and helping others to save face. This is a concept we Americans tend to overlook. And we bear needless pain and inflict needless pain because we underrate this vital aspect of human relations.

Take to heart this saying attributed to Confucius. "Do not talk of a noose in the house of one who was hanged."

You already know how effective it is to talk about subjects of mutual interest with friends and acquaintances. But have you considered the importance of avoiding sore subjects?

What are sore subjects?

Subjects that hurt, and those subjects will vary with the individual. My research tells me there are numerous sore subjects. These are the most frequently mentioned:

- obesity to one who is overweight
- emaciation to one who is noticeably underweight
- height to those who consider themselves too short or too tall (comments about "the weather up there" are not clever)
- marital status to the newly single or to those who'd like to be married but aren't
- age (it is particularly annoying when the interrogator—posing as a friend—asks questions such as, "How old were you when you married?" and then a bit later in the conversation, "How long have you been married?")
- children to the childless
- baldness to those with thinning hair

Be sensitive to other areas of possible soreness: questions about college degrees to those who don't have them, handicaps, job title, salary. Just because a subject is pleasant to you is no assurance that others will find it so.

- Don't withhold honest praise because it's embarrassing for you to give it; people hunger for it.

When competition becomes keen between candidates for jobs or promotions, those with charm get the nod. Many companies consider charm so important they're sending those marked for the heights to "charm school." They make jokes about it; but they go, they learn, and they profit from it.

3. Be *committed*. Those who have commitment, hunger, and drive are the darlings of the corporate world.

When I asked Oscar Welch, executive producer of Miami's "P.M. Magazine," what he looked for in those he hired, he told me, "I want them to have the same slogan as the car, 'I am driven.' I want the person with drive, with commitment."

Commitment means dedicating yourself to all that is necessary to do a superior job. If you need credentials or a degree, go after them.

If you must put in extra time to get the job done, do it. But don't fall into the trap of extra time for its own sake. That just gets you a reputation as a drudge.

Include a concern for profit in your commitment and be constant in your efforts.

4. Be a *communicator*. Learn to express your thoughts in a clear, concise, crisp way. Because we are in a communications explosion, your need to communicate will become increasingly important, not less so.

Look quickly now. I'm about to include a crash course for the communicator.

- Learn the language of your job. Study my glossary of terms but build your own. Start with a list of the hundred most-used words and phrases that have to do with your field of work: management information systems, accounting, real estate, banking, engineering, law, or whatever. When you've mastered these, add another hundred and go on to a third or fourth set as needed.

- Write simply. Write concise memos, letters, and reports using short words, short sentences, and short paragraphs.

An easy test for readability is this: Count the number of words you string together before coming to some sort of break (, . : ; —). If you average more than twenty words before giving your reader a breathing space, you're probably tiring your reader. Aim for an *average* of 10–15 words. For variety's sake, use different lengths for your phrases and sentences.

Try cutting out some of your verbiage. You can lose a lot of words and add zing to your copy by merely eliminating unnecessary "thats." You might also try a "which" hunt and exorcise a few whiches. If you think a sentence or paragraph has to be long to be strong, consider this verse from the Bible: "Jesus wept."

- Practice paraphrasing the writings of someone who has a crisp style. All you need to do is copy a short, well-cast sentence. Then express the same thought in your words. I do this with Ann Landers's material because she's a master of the simple, declarative sentence.

Initially, I used twice as many words to say the same thing Ann did. And I didn't express it half so well. Now I resort to this exercise whenever I find myself becoming wordy.

Try it. It will give your writing vibrancy and tone.

- Have someone you respect monitor your speech and writing. Ask that person to alert you to your abused and misused words as well as to your tired phrases. Then eliminate them. The words and phrases—not the monitor.

Remember, you are "only as good as your word."

5. Be *confident*. Confidence is contagious. The opposite is also true: If you don't believe in yourself, no one else will.

Your overall composure can lend an aura of confidence. Look people in the eye when communicating with them, whether as a talker or as a listener.

If you are nervous, wiggle your toes inside your shoes; this will keep you from more distracting habits such as foot tapping or nail biting.

Self-esteem—confidence—is the golden ingredient in success. If you believe you will succeed, you will. Make this self-fulfilling prophesy work *for* you.

6. Be *creative.* Discover your unique talents and use those talents in creative ways. You might develop a specialty that contributes to your organization's prestige or growth. Look to those areas of your interests and talents that logically coincide with your work. If you relate well to college students, offer to add recruiting to your duties. This could provide you with the low-risk environment necessary to develop your speaking skills as well as provide the opportunity to travel and to keep up with the educational aspects of your career field.

It's so easy to let others douse your creativity. Don't. Robert Ingersoll once said, "College is the place where pebbles are polished and diamonds are dimmed." Diamonds can be dimmed in the work setting as well.

Remember, it's the discretionary aspects of your job that make you shine and lead you to power, not the aspects of your job with the rules and routine.

Creative ideas are not enough; you will need to be creative about the way you sell those ideas.

7. Be *current.* Know what is going on in the world and know how your organization is affected. Let your employer know you value currency and have a breadth of interest. Also, that you're not afraid of machines that make your life easier.

In order to communicate your currency to your boss, you'll need to include in your reading those publications your boss reads.

Point yourself toward tomorrow and your company will include you in tomorrow's plans.

10

COMING TO TERMS:

A GLOSSY GLOSSARY

I went to a lot of trouble to include this glossary of abbreviations and terms because I hope to spare you the embarrassment of feeling out-of-it—as I've felt on a number of occasions—when I didn't understand the conversation going on about me.

Please don't bandy these terms about in order to show how informed you are. You'll risk making some other soul feel out-of-it.

True communicating means *exchanging* thoughts or messages with someone else; to do that effectively both sender and receiver must understand the words used in the exchange.

GENERAL BUSINESS TERMS

abstract: a summary of important points

ACD: automatic call distributor—part of the telephone or other equipment that automatically dials into a terminal or to another telephone

ad hoc: with respect to a particular thing, for a specific purpose, case, or situation; often an ad hoc committee is formed to carry out a specific item on an agenda

ADP: automatic data processing

ad val/ad valorem: according to value (Latin)

AP: Associated Press

ASAP: as soon as possible

BBA: Bachelor of Business Administration

BBB: Better Business Bureau

B/L: bill of lading

BSc: Bachelor of Science

BTU: British thermal unit

CCTV: closed circuit television

CD: certificate of deposit

CEO: chief executive officer

CFA: chief financial analyst

CFO: chief financial officer

CIF: central information file; also, cost, insurance, and freight—the sender is responsible for the goods until they arrive safely at their final destination

COD: cash on delivery

COLA: cost-of-living adjustment

consignment: goods given to another for sale

consortium: a group that pools its resources (financial or otherwise)

CORE: Congress of Racial Equality

COS: cash on shipment; also, chief of staff

CPA: Certified Public Accountant

CPI: consumer price index—a monthly measure, put out by the federal government, of selected goods and services consumed by individuals

DBA: doing business as

debenture: a bond backed solely by the credit standing of the issuer—no assets are pledged as security

demurrage: detention of a ship, freight car, or other cargo conveyance during loading or unloading beyond the scheduled time of departure, or the compensation paid for this detention

DOT: Department of Transportation; also, Dictionary of Occupational Titles

EDP: Electronic Data Processing

EEOC: Equal Employment Opportunity Commission

E-mail: electronic mail

entrepreneur: someone who starts and manages a business enterprise; lately, this word has taken on a broader meaning—it can refer to someone who is in charge of a specific part of the business within a large organization

EOM: end of month

equity: the value of a property or business after any liability against it has been deducted; also, investments that signify ownership (stocks) as opposed to indebtedness (bonds) are referred to as equities

ERISA: Employee Retirement Income Security Act

est: Erhard Seminars Training, a philosophical movement started by Werner Erhard

ETA: estimated time of arrival

exempt employee/non-exempt employee: refers to whether or not an employee is subject to the provisions of the wage and hour law

fast track: what you are on if your boss is moving you at a rapid clip

FCC: Federal Communications Commission

FDA: Food and Drug Administration

FICA: Federal Insurance Contributions Act

FIFO: first in, first out

FITW: Federal Income Tax Withholding

flextime: an arrangement whereby the employer and employee agree on flexible working hours

FM: frequency modulation

FOB: free on board—the sender is responsible for the goods until they are safely on board the truck, plane, train, or ship

franchise: an agreement between a manufacturer and a distributor or dealer to sell the manufacturer's goods or products on an exclusive basis within the territory

FRS: Federal Reserve System

FTC: Federal Trade Commission

FX: foreign exchange

FYI: for your information

FY: fiscal year

GAAP: generally accepted accounting procedures

garnishment: a legal attachment to an employee's wages to pay a debt owed to someone other than the employer

glitch: snag, snarl, error

Glyme's Formula for Success: The secret of success is sincerity. Once you can fake that, you've got it made.

GNP: gross national product

golden handshake/golden parachute: terms used to refer to the separation settlement or early retirement package offered to a long-term employee

Gresham's Law: Bad money pushes good money out of circulation.

Gresham's Law of Projects: Trivial projects tend to displace the more demanding but more worthwhile projects.

Gumperson's Law: If nothing can possibly go wrong, something will.

hands on: usually used as "hands-on experience"; it means the actual experience of doing the work

headhunter: slang expression for executive search consultant, someone who finds appropriate executives for specific job openings within a client corporation

human resources: this is the field of work we used to refer to as "personnel"; it encompasses much more than the hiring and firing of personnel

IRA: individual retirement account

IRS: Internal Revenue Service

ITC: International Trade Commission

jobber: a person who buys from a producer and sells to a retailer

journeyman: a fully qualified crafts worker, generally one who has mastered the trade by serving an apprenticeship

Keogh: a tax-deferred investment for a self-employed person

LCL: less than carload lot

LIFO: last in, first out

"line" manager: usually has direct responsibility for results (see "staff" manager)

L*S*I*T*T: let's stick it to them

M & A's: mergers and acquisitions

manifest: an itemized list of cargo

MBA: Master of Business Administration

MBO: management by objectives

microfiche: a sheet of microfilm that contains rows of micro-images of pages of printed matter

microfilm: a film upon which documents are photographed and greatly reduced in size

MIS: management information systems; yes, managing these systems is called MIS-management

Murphy's Law: If anything can go wrong, it will.

NLRB: National Labor Relations Board

OAG: Official Airline Guide

OSHA: Occupational Safety and Health Act

outplacement: placement help for the person on the way "out"

Pareto's Law: Twenty percent of anything takes eighty percent of application.

Parkinson's Law: The task expands to meet the time available for its completion.

Parkinson's Corollary: Expenditures rise to meet and slightly exceed income.

PBX: private branch exchange

perk: perquisite—a reward or privilege provided in addition to your regular salary; membership in a country club is an example

The Peter Principle: People in organizations tend to rise to their level of incompetence.

P & L: profit and loss

pro rata: in proportion

prospectus: a formal summary of a proposed venture

quality circles: a Japanese management innovation to involve non-management people in operational decisions; essentially the same principle as participative management with work teams

QC: quality control

QED: quod erat demonstratum—which was to be demonstrated (Latin)

quid pro quo: an equal exchange or substitution—something for something

R & D: research and development

SBA: Small Business Administration

SCORE: Service Corps of Retired Executives

SEC: Securities and Exchange Commission

SIG: special interest group

SOP: standard operating procedure

"skunkworks": referred to in *In Search of Excellence* (see Bibliography) as a small band of mavericks monomaniacally working to get a particular task done. Li'l Abner fans may remember the skunkworks that Earthquake McGoon worked in.

"staff" manager: usually is responsible for support to the "line" function

survivorship: the right of a surviving partner or joint owner to the entire assets that were originally jointly owned

TA: transactional analysis

TVA: Tennessee Valley Authority

TWX: teletypewriter exchange

UPC: Universal Product Code

UPI: United Press International

VIP: very important person

VTR: video tape recorder

WATS lines: Wide Area Telecommunications Service

wpm: words per minute

HELLO, MR. CHIPS

And now, we get technical.

If you're a technophobe—like me—you'll need all the help you can get to understand the ubiquitous computer. So, take this part bit by bit and you won't risk over-"byte."

If you're *into* computers, please don't quarrel with my definitions unless you can simplify them still further.

BASIC: Beginner's All-purpose Symbolic Instruction Code, a programming language developed by Dartmouth College; especially well suited to personal computers and beginning users.

binary code: a number system that use only two digits, 0 and 1. A number or letter can be expressed as a combination of these digits. Computers translate each character of information into a string of binary numbers.

bit: the smallest unit or bit of information; short for binary digit

byte: a single unit of information, or one space in the computer memory—for personal computers a byte is usually eight bits

CAD/CAM: computer aided design/computer aided manufacturing

chip: a waferlike disc of silicon and metal etched with miniature circuitry

COBOL: Common Business-Oriented Language; a programming language that is well suited to business applications involving complex data records and large amounts of printed output

CPU: central processing unit—brains of the system

CRT: cathode-ray tube, like a television screen

curser: humanoid who is trying to learn to operate the computer

cursor: little blinking square, line, or other marker to show you where on the screen the work is being done

data: letters, numbers, facts, and symbols for use by the computer

disk: rigid, flat, circular plate with a magnetic coating for storing data

diskette/floppy disk: flexible, flat, circular plate permanently housed in a paper envelope, with a magnetic coating that stores data; standard sizes are 5¼ or 8 inches in diameter

dot-matrix printer: prints letters and numbers with little dots

encode: to put a message into code

FORTRAN: stands for Formula Translation, a widely used high-level programming language; it is well suited to problems that can be expressed in algebraic formulas—generally used in scientific applications

graphics: refers to diagrams, mathematical drawings, or charts

hacker: someone who plays with computers, particularly someone who attempts the electronic invasion of data bases

hardware: the equipment that makes up a computer system: the keyboard, system box, and monitor (screen) are all hardware components

interface: connecting device; place where two or more independent systems meet and interact with each other; as, the interface between a computer and printer

magnetic media: any of several formats that can record and play back magnetic impulses

mainframe: a computer that is physically large and provides the capability to perform applications requiring large amounts of data, usually accessible from a number of terminals

microcomputer: a computer that is physically very small; personal and home computers are usually microcomputers

minicomputer: a type of computer whose physical size is usually smaller than a mainframe—for small business use

modem: comes from the term modulator/demodulator; a

device that converts computer signals (or data) into high-frequency communications signals, and vice versa; the signals can then be sent over telephone lines

on-line: having direct access to the computer; for example, airline reservation systems are "on-line"

PASCAL: a programming language that can be used on many microcomputers. It is considered more difficult to learn than BASIC but it can generate programs that run faster and use less memory. The name comes from that of the French mathematician and philosopher Blaise Pascal.

printer: the device that produces a paper copy of a document

RAM: Random Access Memory, the type of memory used in most computers to store the data and the instructions of programs currently being run

ROM: Read Only Memory, memory containing fixed data or instructions that are permanently loaded during the manufacturing process; a computer uses the data in ROM, but cannot change it

software: computer programs (business systems, games, etc.) as distinguished from hardware (the computer itself); the instructions that tell a computer what to do

subroutine: in music we have a refrain (a theme that is repeated throughout the work); in computer talk the refrain is called a subroutine

terminal: keyboard plus either a CRT or a printer; a "smart terminal" also has some data-processing capability

text: words

video screen: monitor

VDT: video display terminal

VT: video terminal

word processor: an electronic text-editing system that lets you compose and work with material on a video display screen before printing it

word wrapping: the automatic shifting of words from a line that is too long to the next line

SIGNALS FROM YOUR FRIENDLY SATELLITE

dish: a bowl-shaped antenna to link an earth station with a satellite

downlink: a dish that receives signals from a satellite; the dish must be "tuned" to the satellite, as you would tune a television set to a channel

footprint: the geographic area that can receive satellite signals; it takes three satellites, strategically placed, to "footprint" the world

geostationary orbit: satellites are "parked" 22,300 miles above the earth, moving at the same speed as the earth rotates, so that they appear to stand still

narrowcasting: the opposite of *broad*casting; refers to a program that is geared to a narrow audience (learn this one— you're going to hear it often)

satellite: a communications vehicle put into orbit around the earth, and containing *transponders*, which receive, amplify, and retransmit signals

steerable: an uplink that can be "tuned"—as you would direct a flashlight beam—to hit any satellite

uplink: a dish that transmits signals to a satellite, to be bounced back to a downlink on earth; the transmit-receive process takes one quarter of a second

VF: video frequency; also, visual field

METRIC WON'T GO AWAY

If you already use the metric system in your work, I hope you have a good glossary of metric terms on hand. This isn't it, for a complete glossary would be longer than this book.

If you don't use the metric system in your work and hate the idea of "going metric," gentle yourself along by learning a little at a time. Here's a start.

Length

The basic unit of length in the metric system is the meter. Other common units are the centimeter (1/100 meter) and the kilometer (1,000 meters).

Metric to English
1 centimeter = 0.39 inches
1 meter = 39.37 inches
1 meter = 1.09 yards
1 kilometer = 0.62 miles

English to Metric
1 inch = 2.54 centimeters
1 foot = 30.48 centimeters
1 yard = 0.914 meters
1 mile = 1.61 kilometers

If you've a runner in the house, pay attention when you hear talk of a 10K race (that means the race covers 6.2 miles). If you keep listening, you'll soon be converting kilometers to miles on your own.

Area

The common units of area in the metric system are the square meter, the hectare, and the square kilometer.

Metric to English
1 sq. meter = 10.76 sq. feet
1 hectare = 2.47 acres
1 sq. kilometer = 0.386 sq. miles

English to Metric
1 sq. foot = 0.093 sq. meters
1 acre = 0.405 hectares
1 sq. mile = 2.59 sq. kilometers

Volume

The basic unit of volume in the metric system is the liter, which is the same size whether dry or liquid measure. This eliminates the confusion of the English system in which a dry quart is larger than a liquid quart. The milliliter (1/1000 liter) is also used.

Liquid Measure

Metric to English
1 milliliter = 0.0338 ounces
1 liter = 1.057 quarts
1 liter = 0.264 gallons

English to Metric
1 ounce = 29.57 milliliters
1 pint = 0.474 liters
1 quart = 0.947 liters
1 gallon = 3.789 liters

Dry Measure

Metric to English
1 liter = 0.908 quarts
1 liter = 0.114 pecks
1 liter = .0284 bushels

English to Metric
1 quart = 1.10 liters
1 peck = 8.1 liters
1 bushel = 35.24 liters

Weight

The basic unit of weight in the metric system is the gram. Other common units are the kilogram (1000 grams) and the metric ton (1000 kilograms).

Metric to English
1 gram = .0353 ounces
1 kilogram = 2.205 pounds
1 metric ton = 1.102 tons

English to Metric
1 ounce = 28.35 grams
1 pound = 453.6 grams
1 ton = 0.907 metric tons

Temperature

The Celsius (or Centigrade) scale is considered metric because there are 100 degrees between the freezing and boiling points of water. One degree Celsius equals 1.8 degrees Fahrenheit. Because the two scales do not have zero at the same point, a table is convenient for comparison.

	°F	°C
	−40	−40
	−30	−34.5
	−22	−30
	−20	−28.9
	−10	−23.3
	−4.0	−20
	0	−17.8
	10	−12.2
	14.0	−10
	20	−6.7
	30	−1.1
Freezing point	32	0
	40	4.4
	50	10.0
	60	15.6
Room temperature	68	20.0
	70	21.1
	80	26.7
	86	30
	90	32.2
Body temperature	98.6	37
	100	37.8
	122	50
	150	65.6
	167	75
	200	93.3
Boiling point	212	100
	300	148.9
	392	200

BIBLIOGRAPHY

Adams, David, R., Ph.D.; Wagner, Gerald E., Ed. D.; and Boyer, Terrence J., C.D.P., *Computer Information Systems: An Introduction.* Cincinnati: South-Western Publishing, 1983.

Bach, Marcus, *The World of Serendipity.* Marina Del Rey, Calif.: De Vorss, 1980.

Bennis, Warren G., *The Unconscious Conspiracy: Why Leaders Can't Lead.* New York: AMACOM, 1976.

————, ed. *The Planning of Change.* 3rd ed. New York: Holt, Rinehart & Winston, 1976.

Blake, Robert R., and Mouton, Jane Srygley, *The New Managerial Grid.* Houston: Gulf Publishing, 1978.

Blanchard, Kenneth, and Johnson, Spencer, *The One Minute Manager.* New York: Morrow, 1982.

Bloch, Arthur, *Murphy's Law Book Two.* Los Angeles: Price/Stern/Sloan, 1980.

Cetron, Marvin, and O'Toole, Thomas, *Encounters With the Future: A Forecast of Life in the 21st Century.* New York: McGraw-Hill, 1982.

Crimmins, C. E., *The Official Young Aspiring Professional's Fast-Track Handbook.* Philadelphia: Running Press, 1983.

Deal, Terry, and Kennedy, Allan, *The Rites & Rituals of Corporate Life.* New York: New American Library, 1982.

Digital Equipment Corporation, *Guide to Personal Computing.* New York: Maynard, 1982.

Douglass, Merrill E., and Douglass, Donna N. *Manage Your Time, Manage Your Work, Manage Yourself.* New York: AMACOM, 1980.

Frost, David, with Deakin, Michael, *David Frost's Book of the World's Worst Decisions.* New York: Crown, 1983.

Ginsberg, Sigmund, *Management, An Executive Perspective.* Reston, Virginia: Reston Publishing, 1982.

Harragan, Betty L., *Games Mother Never Taught You.* New York: Warner Books, 1978.

————, *Knowing the Score.* New York: St. Martin's Press, 1983.

Hirsch, Gretchen, *Womanhours.* New York: St. Martin's Press, 1983.

Kahn, Herman, *The Coming Boom*. New York: Simon & Schuster, 1982.

Kolb, David. *Organizational Psychology*. Englewood Cliffs, N.J.: Prentice-Hall, 1984.

Lakein, Alan, *How to Get Control of Your Time and Your Life*. New York: Signet, 1976.

Lynn, Jeffrey, *How to Turn an Interview into a Job*. New York: Simon & Schuster, 1983.

Marsteller, William A., *Creative Management: A Euphemism for Common Sense*. Chicago: Crain Books, 1981.

Martin, Judith, *Miss Manners' Guide to Excruciatingly Correct Behavior*. New York: Atheneum, 1982.

Martin, Phyllis, *Word Watcher's Handbook: A Deletionary of the Most Abused and Misused Words*. New York: St. Martin's Press, 1982.

Maslow, Abraham. *The Farther Reaches of Human Nature*. New York: Viking, 1971.

McDonald, James O., *Management Without Tears*. Chicago: Crain Books, 1981.

McLean, Hugh A., *There Is a Better Way to Manage*. New York: AMACOM, 1982.

McWilliams, Peter A., *The Word Processing Book: A Short Course in Computer Literacy*. Los Angeles: Prelude Press, 1982.

Mitchell, Charlene, with Burdick, Thomas, *The Extra Edge*. Washington, D.C.: Acropolis Books Ltd., 1983.

Molloy, John, *Dress for Success*. New York: Warner Books, 1976.

———, *The Woman's Dress for Success Book*. New York: Warner Books, 1978.

———, *Molloy's Live for Success*. New York: Morrow, 1981.

Montagu, Ashley, *Touching*. New York: Harper & Row, 1978.

Naisbitt, John, *Megatrends*. New York: Warner Books, 1982.

Pascale, Richard, and Athos, Anthony, *Art of Japanese Management*. New York: Simon & Schuster, 1981.

Peters, Thomas J., and Walterman, Robert H., Jr., *In Search of Excellence*. New York: Harper & Row, 1983.

Randolph, Robert M., *Thank God It's Monday*. Englewood Cliffs, N. J.: Institute for Business Planning, 1982.

Roddick, Ellen, *Writing That Means Business*. New York: Macmillan, 1984.

Schwartz, David J., *The Magic of Getting What You Want*. New York: Morrow, 1983.

Stewart, Marjabelle Young, and Faux, Marian, *Executive Etiquette*. New York: St. Martin's Press, 1979.

Valenti, Jack, *Speak Up With Confidence: How to Prepare, Learn and Deliver Effective Speeches*. New York: Morrow, 1982.

Wallechinsky, David; Wallace, Amy; and Wallace, Irving, *The Book of Predictions*. New York: Morrow, 1981.

INDEX

139